And Still the Bird Sings

and still
the bird sings

A Memoir of Finding Light After Loss

Linda Broder

SHE WRITES PRESS

Published 2022
Printed in the United States of America
Print ISBN: 978-1-64742-265-3
E-ISBN: 978-1-64742-266-0
Library of Congress Control Number: 2022913044

For information, address:
She Writes Press
1569 Solano Ave #546
Berkeley, CA 94707

She Writes Press is a division of SparkPoint Studio, LLC.

For Michael, Zack, and Lizzie—who always believed in me

And for Brendan—who showed me how to believe in magic

I

The day after my son died, a bird walked into our house. I always start with the bird, even though I didn't believe at first. I didn't even see the bird that day; I was too afraid. But that tiny sparrow wouldn't leave me alone. It knocked on my door and hopped in my house and showed up in my dreams. It wouldn't stop until it sparked a light within me, and then, something so much more.

The day he walked into our house, my husband, Michael, and I sat at our kitchen table, my fingers brushing the scratches etched into the wood. I had bought the table seven years earlier because our old one was too small for our family of five. This was where we did homework and planned our Disney vacations and played Scattergories. But now, I stared at the untouched platters of sandwiches and salads.

It was the last week in August, a time when my three kids should have been mourning the last days of summer. This was an odd year of grades—Lizzie entering fifth, Zack seventh, and Brendan going into ninth. Plastic bags filled with school supplies were scattered across the kitchen counters, along with the piano lessons I'd prepared for my students.

We'd shopped for new sneakers, and their first-day-of-school outfits waited in their closets. Brendan didn't really care about his—just jeans and a T-shirt—but Zack and Lizzie had spent hours trying on different combinations. They had also insisted on buying everything their teachers recommended, even the index cards and the Styrofoam balls I knew they'd never use.

"I only need a notebook and pen," Brendan had said about his first day of high school.

I wanted to put the bags away, to put my lesson plans downstairs in my piano studio, but I stayed rooted to my chair. I couldn't walk into Brendan's empty room. Every few hours, my mother packed up the platters, snapping plastic lids onto the tray of sandwiches and smoothing tin foil over bowls of salad, preserving food none of us could eat.

Our dog, Snowy, whined and began scratching under the lamp table in the den. Michael's sister Hedy called out to us. "I think Snowy has something."

Michael rose and went into the den to check on her.

"Linda," he yelled. "It's a bird." I jumped up, afraid it would fly near me. I was terrified of birds, ever since I was little and there was one trapped in our chimney for days. When we moved to the quiet suburbs of New Jersey, I wouldn't let Michael hang a birdhouse. I was even reluctant to plant trees at first, in case they attracted birds. But Michael had no fear; he owned an exterminating company in New York City.

He ran back into the kitchen and reached for a pair of potholders. I watched him crawl under the end table in the den. He scooped out the bird and walked into the laundry room. I jerked at the scrape of the window opening. I held my breath until Michael walked back into the kitchen, his footsteps heavy and slow.

He didn't sit down.

"It's Brendan," he whispered, his voice raw and broken. His hands, wrapped in the potholders, were cupped, as if he still cradled the bird. He stared down at them and smiled. "The bird. It's Brendan."

My knees buckled. I fumbled for the chair, my hand gripping the back of it. I still trembled with fear, but now anger burned as well. It was the wonder in his voice. No way could I look down at the empty space between Michael's hands and feel his wonder.

"No," I whispered.

"Yes. It's Brendan," he said and that spark in his voice grew stronger until it touched even the sorrow in his eyes. I stared at him, shaking, and yet part of me yearned to reach out and feel the electric air around him. Maybe, for just a moment, I could let that current of wonder flow through me. But no, I couldn't. I tightened my grip on the chair until my fingers turned white.

He smiled down at his hands, and then pressed them against his heart. "It's Brendan."

"It's Brendan!" he yelled again. "It's Brendan." Again and again. Michael's three sisters and mother came running from the living room and gathered around him, alarmed by his frantic shouts of joy.

"Are you okay, honey?" his mother kept asking.

"The bird," Michael answered. "It's Brendan."

She nodded and wrapped her arm around his and leaned forward, smiling at the empty space between his hands. "It's Brendan," she whispered.

I looked over at my father sitting at the table. His head was tilted as he frowned, shaking his head a little as he tried to understand. My mother never stopped moving. She swept away nonexistent crumbs on the table. I stood frozen behind my chair. Snowy ran into the kitchen and barked. Michael laughed and leaned down, showing Snowy his empty hands. "It's Brendan," he said. He wouldn't stop saying it. "It's Brendan."

Michael told everyone about the sparrow. He told the story to his uncles and my two brothers, to anyone who came into the house. His mother kept asking to hear the story again, her eyes wide with wonder. He kept his voice hushed and humbled, as if this bird were a legend thousands of years old. He told the story the same way each time. The bird never grew bigger; there wasn't a flash of light or a crack of thunder when he realized it must be a sign from Brendan. He didn't need to exaggerate; the story was enough for him.

It ended the same way each time, with his hands over his heart, his eyes closed as he let out a long, gentle sigh, before whispering, "It's Brendan."

When all in the house had sighed with him, he flung open the front door and told neighbors, strangers, even the mailman on our block. Everyone listened, of course. Who could say no to a desperate, grieving father?

I watched through the window when he flagged down a neighbor walking her dog. By now, I knew the way his body moved through each part of the story. He bent to scoop up the bird. Even from the house, I saw his face change when he looked down at the bird. My stomach tensed, but I couldn't look away. When he finally pressed his hands to his heart, I did as well. And when he came to the end of the story, I joined in on that long sigh, my breath hissing out of me, unaware I was holding it.

This is what I remember from those early days: Michael ran toward the light. He pushed through the pain drowning him and opened the front door. He spread his arms wide and welcomed hope.

Me? I stayed locked inside, my nose pressed against the glass. I watched—I couldn't look away—but always from a distance, holding my breath, too afraid to touch the light. Even when more birds came and then the songs, and then, oh, so much more, I shook my head no.

But Michael kept holding onto the light. He offered it to me, waiting, waiting, waiting, until it finally moved within me, until I finally believed I deserved the light shining inside me. And, once I did, it changed everything.

Everything.

I believed in the wonders all around me. I believed in magic.

I believed in my son.

2

I was at a tea party on that last Tuesday in August. I stood in my mom's kitchen, watching my daughter Lizzie place teapots on the table. It was the perfect day for a tea party, those last golden days of summer, before school started for my three children, and the piano lessons I gave in my basement studio started up again.

I'm not even sure Lizzie liked tea, but she loved planning the party and setting the table and the idea of three generations sipping tea. She was named after my sister, Elizabeth, who died when she was twelve and I was fourteen. I swore I'd never use a nickname for my daughter, only the full Elizabeth to honor my sister. But when I held her in my arms and looked down at her, she had her own spark, her own shimmer that said *Lizzie*. Still, she shared my sister's giggle and the way she bubbled over with excitement and used ten words when only one was needed.

My father was getting ready to leave. Last year, he'd played the butler, wearing a suit and tie my mother picked out for him. He'd stood straight, a few inches over six feet, despite the emphysema destroying his remaining lung. Lung cancer had stolen the other one. He had an oxygen tank strapped to his back, but still, he bowed to my giggling daughter as he poured her tea, speaking in a silly British accent.

She was ten now, old enough to do it herself. Lizzie had talked about this party for weeks. She danced around the table, her dress flaring out as she straightened the china plate piled with cucumber sandwiches and shining the silver my mother had already polished. I was dressed in my usual leggings and shirt, but my mother had an outfit on. She wore white slacks and red lipstick that exactly matched the red stripes on her shirt and white shoes, since it was still nearly a week before Labor Day. She always followed the rules of fashion.

It was a moment of perfection, the kind you'd post on Instagram. Pastel teapots, lemon bars sprinkled with powdered sugar, and Lizzie skipping around, her brown curls bouncing on her shoulders. She was filled with happiness.

I have no photograph of that day, but that moment is etched deep inside me. The last second before Zack called and we rushed to the hospital. Before rumors swirled around us, and the police kept pulling us aside, asking questions we couldn't answer. This was the Before.

A few months later, my mother returned the tea pots, forgotten in the panic of that day. She washed them, of course, even though they hadn't held tea. She packed them carefully in the wooden crate I'd carried them in, tucking in towels around those perfect tea fairies, dressed in pastel colors.

I threw them all away, even the wooden crate and the towels protecting them.

I rarely rushed my kids to the doctor. My mother-in-law Fran would flinch over the first sign of sickness—a runny nose, a fever—but I'd wave it away, knowing it was probably a virus. Maybe it was the small bit of knowledge I learned those years when my mother dragged me along to the doctor and hospital for my sister, until I was fourteen and we discovered the limits of modern medicine. For a few years after that, I wanted to be a doctor. *You're going to be the one that cures cancer* friends scrawled in my high school yearbook. Instead, I chose music and teaching, knowing that doctors didn't have most of the answers.

So when one of my kids showed signs of sickness, I'd wait, watchful, but not worried. I knew when it was serious, though. I took Zack in to see the doctor right away the time he had a strange rash that landed him in the hospital. I didn't wait for an appointment the time Lizzie woke from a nap, her face flushed with fever from pneumonia. And when Brendan cried out, his crooked arm dangling by his side, I carried him to the car, nine months pregnant with Lizzie, and drove to the emergency room.

I always knew when to call for help.

Except, of course, for that last Tuesday in August.

In those early days of loss, Michael and I built fires. Behind our shed were branches and logs from the pear tree he and Brendan had cut down that last summer. The pile was still a wild tangle of limbs and twigs.

Michael dragged a heavy branch through the grass. He chopped it into smaller pieces and tossed them into the fire pit. We sat in the wooden chairs around the fire. It was still September, but grief made us shiver. We wrapped ourselves in sweatshirts and blankets, feeling the cold no matter how hot the fire burned. Michael wore a baseball cap since he had no hair to keep him warm. Some days, the wind bit into us, but it was our countdown, our dissection of those last minutes before we raced to the hospital that chilled us. We sat around the fire and ran through that morning, staring at the flames, fueled by guilt.

It was my job to convince Michael we'd done nothing wrong. I used logic and my calm teaching voice, the same rational voice I had used to calm Zack down on the phone. I even used props; I dipped a twig into ashes and drew a timeline of that morning on the stone ledge surrounding the fire pit.

Each time, I started with Zack's call.

Zack had left me three messages that morning, only seconds apart. There was no need to panic. *He does this all the time,* I thought, stabbing my stick into the stone ledge and drawing a smudged bullet point. He was almost thirteen and always left me messages. Most of them were about finding his basketball jersey or complaining that Brendan wouldn't share his video game. They were brothers who loved to tease each other. Especially Zack. He'd make up silly phrases that infuriated Brendan like "Oh, my scouche de bouche." Once he left me a series of messages telling me Brendan wouldn't stop looking at him.

I drew a bullet point on my timeline. *There is no need to panic.*

I'd called Zack back, thinking this was a plea for them to have jalapeño chips and Mountain Dew soda at lunch. Maybe even ice cream.

"I can't find Brendan," he said, his voice thin and breathless.

And still, I didn't panic.

Michael hunched over the fire now, the flames drawing shadows on his narrow face. He poked at the logs with a thick stick. "That's when we should have called the police."

Zack had called Michael at work. For five minutes or so on that day, we'd both known Zack couldn't find his brother, and still we stayed calm. Sparks from the fire shot into the air; I waited until they settled before continuing with our defense.

Of course, I should have called the police. My son had called and whispered his brother was missing. Instead, I gave Zack a list of places to check. An hour before, when I'd left the house, Brendan was clacking away at his computer, lost in his virtual game world.

"He's probably taking a break," I said to Zack on the phone. "Check the backyard. The deck."

My mind never leapt to horror, only logical explanations. He was out walking the dog. Maybe playing a trick on his brother, trying to scare him.

"I checked all those places," Zack said. His footsteps echoed in the background, moving faster as he paced. I held my hand over the phone. My father was just about to leave the tea party; I sent him to check on the boys.

I still wasn't worried. A little nervous, but mostly for the panic I heard in Zack's voice. That's a mark against me. I had such innocent thoughts. *Maybe he's in his closet, waiting to pounce on Zack. Playing a prank on his brother.*

"Check his room again," I said.

"I can't," he whispered. "His door is blocked by something. I can see fur under the crack. I think it's a dog."

The dog.

The dog haunted us now. Sitting by the fire, Michael and I stayed on this part a long time. Sometimes, I drew the dog as an X on the timeline. Sometimes it was a bullet point. But never a checkmark, never something good. Michael walked to the back of the shed, dragging another log over to the fire.

"That damn dog," he said, as if it were real. If only it had been real. Michael picked up the ax lying on the grass. His legs had the lean lines of a runner, but his shoulders were thick with muscles. Rage gave him even more power. He swung the ax and hacked through the wood, little chunks flying through the air. "We should've called the police then."

But for a few minutes that day, we really thought it was a dog trapped in Brendan's room. He loved animals. He had no fear of them. He was the one who poked the dead possum and then wrapped him in a plastic bag. He hunted for the groundhog hiding under our shed. He grabbed a broom with his cousin Sean and chased a chipmunk around our house, Brendan lifting up couches with ease. Oh, how they'd laughed that day, Sean amazed at Brendan's strength. It seemed reasonable that he'd found a stray dog and brought him into his room, maybe with a bowl of water, and then walked around the neighborhood looking for the owners. Scaring his little brother would have been an added bonus.

We never wondered that Tuesday morning why Zack didn't start with the dog, and oh, that's a black mark against us. I dipped my stick in ashes and scratched an X on our stone ledger. We never wondered why our own dog wasn't barking and scratching, trying to get to this imaginary dog. We latched onto the idea of a dog, an explanation that seemed reasonable. Logical.

I'd called my neighbor Patty two doors down to check on Zack that morning. This was a point in our favor. I put a checkmark on our timeline. This is what a good parent would have done, right? Call a friend to check on her sons, even when she was still convinced a dog was in Brendan's room.

"Do you want me to break down the door?" she'd asked. I hesitated for a half a second. *This is a joke gone wrong. Tonight, we'll all be sitting around the dinner table, laughing over the stupid joke Brendan played on his brother.*

I'd said yes, but I counted that half second against me on our timeline. It's not a bullet point, but an *X*, a black stain against the stone. Michael added an armful of leaves to the fire. We watched the flames lick at the leaves until they curled and disappeared into smoke. We needed more fire for this part, more ashes.

My father had arrived at my house. We still hadn't called the police. Michael was in his office in New York City. I was in my mother's kitchen, waiting. Frozen. That's another *X* on the stone. Why did I just stand in the kitchen, waiting, staring at the perfect row of pictures on my mother's fridge? Why didn't I rush home? Instead, I sent my father, a man battling emphysema with a tank of oxygen strapped to his back. I don't even think I told him to rush.

The marks on the timeline were closer together now, each *X* bleeding into the next one.

My mother no longer walked around the table setting up, pretending everything was fine. She stood by her phone, one hand on it, waiting for a signal from me. There was no screaming or crying; we stayed calm for Lizzie. She even smiled at her, as if everything were fine. We stayed strong.

My neighbor had called me back. Her voice was clipped. Scared. Fear swirled inside me, but still, I didn't panic. I stayed strong. I nodded at my mother and she understood my code. She picked up the phone and called the police.

"Please, hurry," she said. "This is a child."

My father ran into our house. Despite the tank strapped to his shoulder, he raced up the stairs and pushed against Brendan's blocked door. When it didn't move, he sank to the floor and reached into the crack with his fingers, breathing hard as he gasped for air. He felt the brown fur that had frightened Zack. A minute later, paramedics burst up the stairs and through Brendan's door, taking away our last shred of hope.

This wasn't a prank. It wasn't an animal lying on the floor, trapped inside.

It was Brendan.

Michael and I spent months on that morning, debating the ifs, onlys, and should haves. We collected them like the dried leaves scattered on our grass. We burned them in the fire, watched them singe, curl, and melt away. The fire eased some of our guilt, but then, those lines I scratched into stone were easy to erase. Even the shadow of the ashes washed away in the rain.

For me, the timeline of that morning was the small wound, one that burned fast and quick like the dried leaves in flame. It's not the morning that scarred me, but the days, the months before that haunted me. Those wounds were bigger than the branches Michael dragged through the grass. The things I'd said and the things I never said outweighed the heavy logs behind the shed, the ones too wide to wrap my arms around, the ones I couldn't even lift.

I didn't offer my sins to the fire before me; I didn't want absolution. I didn't deserve it. I kept it all inside, buried deep, like the embers hidden beneath ash, waiting for that whisper of wind to stir it all into flames and consume me once again.

3

My mother, Lizzie, and I rushed to the hospital. It was a twenty-minute drive, and we said almost nothing. My mother and I built a wall around our fear. I'd learned from her the power of pushing away pain and fear. There were no tears, not even a quiver in my voice when I turned to Lizzie. I smiled at her, squeezing her hand. I might have joked, trying to reassure her. I was good at it; she swung her legs back and forth, as if this ride were part of the tea party. My mother drove, her hands clutching the steering wheel, her knuckles blanched white.

"It might be diabetes," she said at one point. "That runs in our family."

I latched onto that idea, holding it tight. It was a logical explanation, something that could be fixed. Brendan didn't play soccer or join in on the football games a few houses down like Zack did. He spent his afternoons at his desk, doing homework and playing video games. His eyes never leaving the screen, he'd pull open his drawer and reach for a pack of fruit gummies.

"Don't worry, Mom. They have fruit in them. They have to be healthy," he'd say and dump an entire pack into his mouth. Except for the yellow ones. Those he saved for his sister.

I didn't wait for my mother to park. I ran into the emergency room. The nurse at the desk told me they hadn't brought him in yet.

My muscles melted in relief. *If it were an emergency, he'd be here by now.* I glanced at the others in the waiting room. I didn't know their stories, but mine wasn't serious.

The woman at the desk told me to take a seat. *Another good sign. If it were an emergency, they'd rush me into his room.* I sat on one of the hard plastic chairs lining the emergency room and built myself a fantasy. He was sitting up in the ambulance right now, making jokes, his cheeks stained red as he tried deflecting all the attention away from him.

It's diabetes. I looked down at the floor, taking deep breaths, but my gaze kept turning to the woman next to me. She sat there, her hair tangled around her face, her legs splayed out. She kicked them back and forth while her fingers tapped the chair. Her rhythm was jerky and syncopated, and I couldn't seem to breathe. My eyes kept blurring.

It's that damn tapping. Why won't she stop tapping?

I didn't hear the nurse walk toward me until she stood over me and brushed her hand on mine. "You can come in now," she said softly and I jumped up. My mother was still parking, but I knew she'd find me. She knew her way around hospitals. The woman next to me jumped up too.

"Hey," she said. "How come she gets to go in before me? I was here longer. And I'm sicker than she is."

The nurse ignored her and took my arm, guiding me away from the room. She barely touched me, but her grip felt like a vise.

The woman started shouting. "It's not fair. I was here first. Why is she so lucky? She's so lucky."

I had the strangest urge to shake off the nurse's arm and apologize. I wanted to pull away and tell this screaming woman she could go first, that of course, her problem was worse than my son's. He's laughing in the ambulance right now. He has diabetes. That can wait. But the nurse pulled me down the maze of hallways into a small room filled with chairs. She left and I let out the air in my lungs, still hearing the woman's screams. This wasn't an exam room, but a quiet place to talk about a treatment plan for diabetes. All I needed to do was sit in one of these chairs and wait for Michael. He was coming in from the city; it would be at least another hour. But we had time. Hospitals were slow, and we'd probably be here all afternoon. Eventually, they'd bring in a case worker and a dietitian, and together we'd learn how to manage his diabetes.

It's going to be okay. I am *the lucky one. I'll stop buying gummy worms, even the ones with all fruit. I'll make a plan and practice giving insulin shots to an orange.*

I sat in the chair, letting the calm fill me. I'd never given shots before, but I could handle it. I was strong. I'd been in the emergency room many times with the kids for broken bones, stitches, even a concussion. When Zack was three, I'd brought him into the emergency room with the back of his head bleeding. Brendan had swung a baseball bat, unaware his brother had crept up behind him. They wanted to bundle a crying Zack onto a papoose board. I took one look at the straitjacket attached to the board and shook my head.

"I'll keep him calm," I said to the nurse.

She shook her head. "He's going to jerk his head. He needs three staples so we'll have to restrain him."

But I knew I was enough to soothe him. I placed Zack on my lap, took a deep breath and wrapped my arms around him. I breathed into his neck, slow and deep, letting my calm settle over him. When his breathing slowed, I nodded and the doctor came closer and quickly squeezed the stapler into the back of his head. *One. Two. Three.*

Zack whimpered with each staple. I grimaced, but we never

moved. I stayed strong and helped my son. That's exactly what I'd do with Brendan's needles. We'd figure it out together.

I closed my eyes for a moment, leaning into the chair, blocking out the sounds around me. But the screech of an ambulance shattered my peace. I opened the door. I stepped into the hallway. The paramedics rushed in, wheeling a stretcher. I couldn't see their patient, only his bare feet, but I knew it was Brendan.

He wasn't sitting up or laughing or playing a game on his phone. He was lying down, and oh, my God, someone was on top, kneeling on Brendan, pumping her hands against his heart. They didn't bring him into the quiet room; they pushed into an exam room filled with doctors and nurses and beeping machines. I trailed after them, walking in a trance, half expecting the nurse to grab my arm and guide me away. My eyes never left my son. The top of his head was visible now.

He's not moving.

Doctors and nurses ran around him, yelling things I didn't understand. I wanted Brendan to move, even a twitch of his foot. Anything. Someone grasped my elbow and I looked down at a small man, dressed all in black. Around his neck was a white collar.

A priest. I shook my head. *Why is there a priest in this room with me?*

He squeezed my elbow and nodded at me, but, still I didn't understand. I wanted to go back to the quiet room or even back to the waiting room next to the tapping woman who screamed I was lucky.

Why is he standing so close to me? Why is he holding onto me? Tremors raced through my arms and legs. This wasn't the touch of a priest welcoming you to service. This was one of comfort. Support.

Oh, my God.

I stared down at him, suddenly realizing he'd been in the quiet room with me.

They brought me into a private room with a priest. I didn't notice because I was too busy building my fantasy. I was too busy proving I was strong and could handle this crisis. I'd never even noticed the priest sitting next to me. Still, I stayed strong. I stood tall, not saying a single word.

He reached out and held my elbow, trying to prop me up as if I were going to fall. I tried shifting away, but my feet were trapped in quicksand. The hospital room was big and bright but felt small and dark. Too many people hovered over my son. They never glanced my way, never offered answers to the questions I couldn't push through my lips. They were too busy trying to get my son to breathe. I started counting how many were in the room, but I couldn't focus, especially with the priest standing at my side.

I inched my arm away from him, but his hand stayed, cupping the air between us. He was much shorter than me, and yet strong enough to keep me frozen there, even when he wasn't touching me. He mumbled something and at first I thought he was praying, but, gradually his words pierced my fog.

"Is this your son?"

"How old is he?"

His voice was low, as if we were whispering in the confessional and he was waiting to hear my secrets.

"What's his name?"

"Is your husband coming soon?"

He kept asking me these questions and, finally, frustrated with his distractions, I spat out one word answers. I just wanted him to shut up.

"Fifteen."

"Brendan."

"Soon."

I could barely see Brendan through the wall of nurses surrounding him. Next to his gurney was a digital clock, with red numbers ticking minutes and seconds. I focused on those numbers, time ticking by, absurdly grateful for each second.

A nurse ran to one of the carts, and now I could see more of Brendan. There was a sheet draped over him, twisted high, revealing his bare legs. I jerked my gaze back at the clock, almost embarrassed at his legs. They were sturdy and strong, peppered with dark hair. They weren't the baby legs I'd kissed and tickled after his bath. They weren't the skinny legs of a ten-year-old hiking the mountains of Vermont or even the legs of a thirteen-year-old biking the trail. These were the legs of a man.

When did that happen?

I shivered at the goosebumps on my arms. The priest kept asking me questions. He wouldn't shut up. I had my own questions. *What happened? Why isn't he breathing? Is he going to be okay?*

At that moment, though, I could only focus on a simple fact: Brendan wasn't wearing socks. Brendan loved socks, even as a baby, even in the summer, even at the beach. He lost a toenail when he was four and socks became this protective layer he insisted on. Just the week before, he'd slipped on a pair of thick, woolen socks Michael had bought him for their weekend camping in the snow. I laughed. "It's August. Way too hot for those."

He shrugged, a dismissive one he'd perfected long before he became a teenager. "They're comfy. And you know I hate cold toes."

His feet were bare now, with a hint of blue shading his toes. *They must be cold.* I looked over my shoulder at the cabinets lining the wall. I tried moving to search for extra sheets or socks. This was something I could do to help my son. I had to get socks, but the priest moved closer, squeezing my elbow and blocking my way. I couldn't escape from him and those damn questions he kept asking.

"Please," I whispered and for a moment, he stopped mumbling to listen, but I wasn't talking to him. "Please."

No one stopped or turned around. I didn't even know who I was begging. The doctors. Brendan. Maybe even God. No one listened, but the priest moved even closer.

He dragged a chair behind me. "Why don't you sit?"

I shook my head. He didn't care. He slid the chair until it touched the back of my knees. I sat down, hoping he'd go away, but he only moved behind me, his hands resting on the chair.

I could hear him breathe. He was too close. I jumped up and kicked the chair away. And he only moved closer.

"You're so strong," he murmured. His hand latched onto my elbow. I clenched my fists, fighting the urge to whirl around and hit him. Part of me hated that I was so strong. I was the mother. I was supposed to be screaming and crying, falling to the ground. Or rushing the doctor, tugging on his arm, begging him to save my son.

But I was strong. I stood there tall, my face composed, shaking only on the inside. I watched the numbers on the clock. I didn't ask a single question.

"You're so strong," the priest murmured again.

God, how I hated him.

4

I grew up believing. My body absorbed the rituals of a Catholic mass before I even understood them. I knew when to kneel, when to stand, when to dip into the font of holy water and cross myself, shivering when drops of holiness trickled down my neck. I never rubbed away the drops. I loved the idea of the sacred melting into my skin.

We lived a block away from our church. Every Sunday, my mother laid out our church clothes, even for my father. She loved to dress up and was disappointed when hats and gloves went out of style. My two older brothers, Jimmy and Allan, wore slacks and a collared shirt, with wide stripes that were fashionable in the seventies. My mother liked to sew and made matching dresses for me and my sister, Elizabeth, with pearled buttons and touches of lace. I was ten and had a fur muff, with white rosary beads slipped inside.

We walked to church, our own parade of six. We arrived early so we could slip into the pew my mother claimed as ours. My brothers and I fought not to be the first one in; no one wanted to sit on the end and shake hands with a stranger. Most of the time, I was bored and watched the old ladies, the ones who sat in the middle of the church, their heads draped with black lace, rosary beads dripping from their fingers. Their lips moved in unending prayer. When they'd fingered each bead, they circled around and started all over again.

The organist played the opening chords and I snapped to attention. This was my reward. I loved to sing, especially on my swing set in the backyard. I pumped my legs, moving higher until the swing set started to rock out of the cement holding it to the ground. I sang, feeling the wind move around me, adding its own harmony. My father loved to sing too. Each time we stood to sing in church, he pushed back his shoulders and expanded his ribs. His voice rang out, a loud baritone that made little kids giggle and babies turn around, their eyes wide. He smiled, as if he, too, were on that swing, feeling the wind all around him. I tried to match him with my thin soprano.

Each time we got to my favorite part of the hymn—the Amen— I opened my mouth wide and let the *Ahhh* flow out of me in one long breath. The organist held the chord, drawing out the first part of the Amen. The music swelled inside me, building suspense. I leaned forward, moving onto my toes, my stomach wrapped in knots, waiting for the second half of the Amen.

It felt like riding the wooden roller coaster at Coney Island, each *clickety-clack* drawing me closer to the mountaintop of God, inch by inch, before teetering on the top just for a second. The organ filled the church and that space inside me. I stood on my tippy toes, holding onto that *Ahhh* as long as I could. Finally, the organist moved into the final chord and the second half of the Amen burst out of me, carrying me down the mountain in one long *swoosh*. The chord trailed off, and I ended on a long, soft sigh, safe once again.

5

The priest in the hospital kept trying to get me to sit down. I mostly stared at the clock next to the hospital bed that day, but I couldn't keep track of the numbers. I didn't want to see the backs of the nurses and doctors hunched over Brendan or his bare legs and cold feet. I needed to see his face, so loved, so familiar.

So much of me was in his face. He had my blue eyes and my brown hair. His hair sprouted in all different directions and, on the back of his head was a cowlick, which I used to play with when he was a baby. I tried taming the swirl as he grew older, slicking it down with gel, but, within minutes, it would spring back up, laughing at me. Whenever he unleashed another sarcastic comment, his mouth twisted into a smirk. Also all me.

From Michael he got his insatiable appetite and his long, lean muscles. And his absurd sense of humor. They shared a giant repertoire of private jokes that mostly involved nuts and meat. He was the best of both of us and yet, there was so much that was just him, that made him our son, our Brendan. I needed to see that.

I moved forward. The priest let me go, no longer worried I'd fling myself onto Brendan. I stepped to the right.

I need to see his face. Then everything will be all right. I shifted a little more. *There. Brendan's face.*

My breathing slowed. I held onto this image of my son instead of the doctors and the paddles they kept putting on his chest. I ignored the beeps and the shouted commands and the way his body jerked into the air. I stared at my son. His glasses were gone.

He never let me see him without his glasses, not since fifth grade.

Once when he was thirteen, I snuck into his room when he was sleeping, just to see his face without his glasses. He must have heard me because he was sitting up with his glasses on in the dark.

"Did you need something, Mother?" he teased with a smile.

It became our game. Sometimes, I waited outside the bathroom while he finished showering. He'd open the door, wrapped in a towel, his glasses all steamed up. He couldn't see through the fog, but he'd nod at me and walk toward his room, his hand brushing against the wall to guide him.

I moved farther from the priest. I needed to be closer to Brendan. He looked as if he were sleeping. For a second, I thought he was smiling, maybe even dreaming. But my eyes were too blurred with tears. I rubbed them away. My fingers itched to run through his hair, something he'd never let me do when he was awake.

I moved an inch forward. My hands shook with the need to touch him. I put my hands behind my back. My fingers grabbed onto each other, and I dug my nails into the backs of my hand, carving out tiny wounds.

I moved a step closer.

And that's when I saw the ring of bruises around his neck.

6

The first thing people noticed about Brendan were his eyes. They were the color of the sky, an endless blue that drew you in, with a thick frame of eyelashes he inherited from his father. When he was a baby, strangers would lean into his stroller, captivated by his eyes. If they lingered for a moment, the next thing they noticed was his stare. He loved to stare. I used to wedge him between pillows and prop a black-and-white cloth book in front of him, convinced I was raising a reader. For hours, he sat with me, barely moving, staring at books until he fell asleep.

Even once he was crawling and walking and had a playpen filled with toys, he loved to stare. He'd line up his elephant and tiger and hippo in a row on the coffee table and then sit back and stare at them, his hand tugging on the cowlick at the back of his head. Sometimes, he'd hold one in his hand, rotating it slowly, examining it from each angle. But most of the time, he just looked at them. I bought him a jungle mat with palm trees and a watering hole, but he never bothered playing with it. Staring at his animals was enough.

When he was two, a woman stood behind me on a supermarket line. The cashier was new, fumbling as she hunted for the prices of peppers and lettuce. I held Brendan in my arms as he watched her punch in the numbers. The woman behind us reached out and tickled him on the foot.

When he turned to look at her, she cooed and began her mission to make him laugh. She flashed her rings and played peek-a-boo. She scrunched up her lips and blew raspberries in his face and paused, waiting for his giggle.

Brendan didn't look away or duck his face into the crook of my shoulder. He stared at her, an unblinking laser that never wavered. Finally, the woman dropped her hands. "What's wrong with him?" she asked.

"Nothing," I said. "He's just shy. And quiet."

She shook her head and backed away, turning toward her cart.

My cheeks burned. For a moment, I wished Brendan were the kind of baby who smiled at others. I wished others could hear his belly laugh—a contagious laugh he'd inherited from his Papa Ben, the kind that took over his body and made him roll on the floor.

I'd felt the weight of his stare many times, the one that drilled deep inside you. Sometimes, he'd tilt his head for a long moment and then nod, as if saying, *Yes, I finally understand you.* A tiny bob of his head that made you believe he somehow had discovered all your secrets.

He learned not to stare at strangers as he grew older, but he still drifted into his own world. In my favorite picture of Brendan, he's leaning on an ottoman, his eyes dreamy and soft, watching something only he could see.

Lizzie took that picture sometime during his last summer. Zack was usually outside playing baseball or basketball with his friends, but Lizzie loved spending time with Brendan in his room. When my afternoon piano lessons started, she'd run into his room. He'd sit at his desk, doing homework or playing a video game, while she jumped on his bed and spun around in the extra desk chair until she was dizzy. Then she'd grab his phone and take pictures of the two of them.

When the police finally returned his phone, I'd scrolled through it, searching for answers. There were pictures and videos of the two of them, mostly distorted through an app that made them look like they were inside a funhouse mirror.

I found no answers, but I did find that picture of him, lost in his hidden world. Daydreaming, his teachers called it. He spent most of his time in class staring out the window, but since his grades were good, no one seemed to mind.

I'd asked him about that hidden world, maybe a year before he died. I watched him stare out the window for a long time, his body swaying, his mouth curved in a mysterious smile. He seemed so happy, staring at secrets only he could see. I wanted to know what he saw. Was he hypnotized by the trees moving in the wind? Or remembering the pranks he played when he had sleepovers with his cousins Sean and AJ? Perhaps, he was simply wondering what was for dinner that night.

"What do you see?" I finally asked.

He jerked out of his dream world and smiled at me. He shook his head and walked away without saying a word.

7

Michael burst into the hospital room, his eyes darting back and forth between Brendan and me. When I last talked to him, we weren't sure where Brendan was. We were still convinced this was something we'd laugh about, a story we'd trot out years later at family reunions. *Remember the time Brendan captured a stray dog in his room? Zack was so scared until Brendan came back with the owners.* And we'd laugh until we all cried.

"What's going on?" he asked. "Linda, what's going on?"

I had no answers. I grabbed Michael's hand, grateful for an anchor. I didn't bother introducing him to the priest.

"It's not good." My voice was hushed. I didn't want to distract the doctors. Michael said nothing, just stood there, his hand shaking in mine. "There's something—" The words were dust in my throat, thick on my tongue. I bit my lip and pushed the words out. "There's something on his neck."

I whispered this, a shameful secret that burned through my body. Of course, the doctors and nurses knew. The priest behind me probably knew. Brendan and I shared the same pale skin. Underneath the glare of lights, against the backdrop of the white sheets, his bruises flashed like a neon sign. My hand flew up to my own neck as if I could transfer the bruises and take this pain on.

"I think—" But I couldn't make myself say the words. *They think he did this to himself. Oh, my God. What did he do?*

The doctor looked up and saw Michael. He walked over to us. I shook my head. *Please, don't stop.* I looked over at the clock to make sure it was still ticking. The doctor stood in front of us, shaking his head before he even said anything.

No. But I knew. They'd been waiting for Michael. That's why the priest kept asking me if he was coming. They were waiting for Michael to come, for both parents to be in the room so they could give us time to say goodbye.

"I'm so sorry," the doctor said. I focused on his face. It was shapeless; I couldn't even tell if he wore glasses or had a beard. The only thing I could see was the clock. I needed to see the seconds blinking. The clock made no noise, but those seconds pounded inside me, a pulse I could hear, like Brendan's heartbeat next to mine.

"I'm so sorry," the doctor said again. "We've been working on him for a long time." He gave us specifics, how his heart stopped, how his brain was starved without oxygen. He offered us numbers and medical facts, things I normally latched onto, but right then, the only thing I cared about were the seconds ticking on the clock.

The doctor took off his gloves. "He's gone."

The clock still ticked. *There's still hope.* Even with the doctor's words, even with the priest standing next to me again, clasping my elbow again, I held onto hope.

"Please." I shook off the priest and grabbed the doctor's hands. "Don't give up on him. This is our son. Please."

He looked at us for a moment and then nodded. He turned around. Someone pressed against Brendan's chest and they tried again. We stood there watching, waiting, each movement playing in slow motion. I wanted to beg, but I couldn't talk, could only stutter out a *p*, the start of please. The priest started a prayer. *The last rites?* He motioned, making the sign of the cross and this time, I did too, my body responding on its own.

The doctor moved away from Brendan. Michael lunged forward, reaching for Brendan in that last moment before they declared him gone. I stood rooted, staring at the clock. Tears swam before my eyes. The numbers blurred, but still I stared, straining for the sound of those seconds beating inside me.

Nothing.

He was gone.

8

I don't remember the doctors and nurses walking out. I don't remember when the priest let go of my elbow and stopped praying. At some point, they unhooked the cords snaking from Brendan and shut down all the machines. There were no more beeps or frantic commands. Silence filled the room, thick and heavy. It was Michael and me and one nurse in the room. We stood around him, not touching him, not saying anything.

"You can stay here as long as you want," the nurse said. "No one's going to take him away until you're ready."

I tried to imagine when we'd ever be ready. She walked over to Brendan and reached for the sheet, pulling it up over his chest, her fingers smoothing out each tiny wrinkle. She folded the sheet down, a perfect crease across his chest. Her hands were practiced and sure, brisk even, but her face crumpled with the weight of what she was doing.

"He's cold," I whispered. She nodded, and pulled the sheet up higher, before patting his chest one last time and walking out the door. I wanted more than just a sheet on him. I hated my children cold. The year before, while we packed for his camping trip with the Boy Scouts, I kept tucking sweatshirts into his bag. He kept tossing them out and throwing in a bag of chips instead. I didn't care if he was getting enough to eat or if he was having fun; I tossed in my bed at night picturing him shivering inside his sleeping bag. He never got cold, though; he wore shorts to school when it was forty degrees out.

We dragged chairs closer to him and sat there, not saying anything, just looking at our son. Michael draped one arm over his chest, the other holding his hand. I reached out and touched his hand, but pulled back. It was like ice.

Without his glasses, he looked younger than his fifteen years. Michael reached out and stroked his hair.

"He looks different," he said.

"It's his haircut," I said as if that explained everything. It was so short now. Normally, his hair flew in every direction. He never cared enough to tame the wildness with creams or gels.

"He had a haircut yesterday," I told Michael even though he'd seen him the night before. It was part of the kids' countdown ritual to the first day of school. He'd gone first and then walked the mile home, too impatient to wait for his brother and sister to finish, always racing to get to the next thing.

"I'm here if you have any questions," the nurse had said before she closed the door, but we had none. Later, questions would drown us, but right then, we couldn't hold onto the reality in front of us. He wasn't cold or sleeping. We weren't sure how it happened or why or what those marks meant. We never called her back, never even asked her or the doctors a single question that day. Not one. We just sat there, Michael holding his hand, stroking his hair and wondering why he looked so different.

Michael stood up and draped himself over Brendan. My hands were shaking. I tried moving them closer, but I couldn't touch him. I sat there, patting the bed next to him, careful to keep space between us. *Why can't I touch him?*

I couldn't even hold his hand.

We sat next to Brendan until icy shock seeped into our bones, numbing us, tricking us into thinking we were okay. We pushed back our chairs and stood up. I needed Zack and Lizzie. To hold their hands and run my fingers through their hair. I needed their warmth. My father was still at my house, trying to catch his breath. I texted my neighbor, asking her to bring Zack to the hospital.

I opened the door, sticking my head into the hallway. A nurse looked up and quickly walked over to me. "Can I get you anything?" she asked.

"My son. . . ." I started to say.

She put her hand on my arm. "No one is going to take him away. Not until you're ready."

I almost slammed the door shut again. *How will I ever be ready?* I shook my head. "No, I mean my other son. And my daughter. I need to find them."

Michael squeezed past me to call his mother and I wandered the maze of hallways until another faceless nurse took me by the arm and guided me toward the quiet room. My mother stood at the end of the hallway, talking on the phone.

"I'm fine," I said to the nurse. She raised her eyebrows, perhaps surprised by my voice. It was steady now, and I felt this strange sense of pride. *I am strong. I am strong.* I walked toward my mother, gathering strength with each step. The light above her flickered, casting her face first in shadows and then light. Both showed the deep lines of pain carved in her face.

She knows.

My mother's a small woman; by thirteen I towered over her. She straightened as I walked to her, slipping on the armor she'd perfected so many years before. She grew taller with each step I took, strength radiating from her. Her fingers fumbled, snapping the phone shut and we stared at each other, both knowing there was nothing to say.

Finally, I asked, "Where's Lizzie?"

She pointed to the door. "In there. She's with a nurse, eating ice cream." She paused. "She doesn't know anything."

Michael walked up to us and the three of us stood there, staring at each other. Finally, Michael tilted his head toward the door. "We have to tell Lizzie."

I nodded, then took a deep breath and turned to follow him. My mother cried out and grabbed my arm. "Wait." Her mouth moved, searching for the right words. "Be strong," she finally said.

She nodded toward the door. "Be strong for her." Her fingers dug into my arm, pushing her strength into me. She'd never once asked me to be strong when my sister was sick. Not even after she'd died. But I'd learned by watching her hide her tears until she was behind closed doors.

I didn't need her strength. The icy shock had frozen inside me. I turned away and pushed open the door, pasting on a smile for Lizzie. She sat in the chair, bowl in her lap, smudges of ice cream on her cheeks. Her eyes lit up when she saw us.

"I'm having ice cream for lunch," she said, licking her lips, diving into the bowl for more. "Wait until I tell Brendan and Zack. They're going to be so jealous."

Michael sank to his knees before her, draping his arm across her just like he'd done with Brendan. I stood there, as she scooped up ice cream, too engrossed to notice the tears streaming down our faces. *What if I don't tell her? What if we wait a few days, even a few weeks before ripping away her happiness?* But of course, we had to tell her.

I sat down next to Lizzie and wrapped my arm around her

shoulder. At first, she shifted away, holding her bowl toward her, thinking I was about to snatch away her ice cream, but then Michael spoke. She stiffened when she heard Michael's words, spoon frozen midair. A second later, she dropped her spoon into the bowl, tears washing away the ice cream on her face.

That day is a whirlwind, like a box of blurred images from three different puzzles. I'll never be able to piece together a picture that makes sense. But the sounds from that day are sharp and jagged and captured forever inside me, a symphony of horror I can never escape. They're not the sounds of grief, though. I almost think those sounds would be easier to push away. It's not Lizzie's muffled sobs that pull me under. It's the clink of her dropped spoon hitting the bowl. Not Zack's howls—not even when his screams echoed in the hospital hallway—but the soft screech of his rubber sneakers as he slid to the floor and pounded his fists against the tile.

It's not Michael's anguished cry in that quiet room when he pulled out his phone and read his messages, gasping, his face etched in horror. "Oh, my God, I can't. I just can't." He shoved the phone at me and I read the text from his sister Trudy.

I'm so sorry to hear about Linda's dad.

There were two other messages from his sisters Hedy and Eileen, saying the same thing.

"They think it's your father," he whispered. "I told my mother." He shuddered. "I said the words, I said Brendan, but she thinks it's your father who died. Not Brendan." He stood up slowly, shaking his head.

"Oh, my God, I'm going to have to say the words again." He stared at me helplessly. "I have to say the words again."

It's not his cry that pierces me. Or his footsteps as he opened the door and moved into the hallway to call his mother again. It's the sound the door made. First the whoosh as it opened. Then the sigh as it slowly inched back, until finally, it closed.

That's the sound that haunts me—the soft click of a closing door.

Pianoforte

A keyboard musical instrument that can play both soft (piano) and loud (forte). Over time, it was shortened to the word piano. I like the forte part, though. In Italian, forte means strength.

I need control when I play gentle notes. But thundering chords? That requires strength. My arms drop into the keys with their full weight. My muscles tremble until I ache to stop. Still, I keep playing.

I stay strong.

9

Michael spoke about birds once, years before one walked into our house. It was a few months after his father died. He walked into the bedroom and sat down on the bed, watching me for a long time. Finally he spoke. "I think a bird is watching me."

I shivered. "That's so creepy."

He laughed. "Maybe I shouldn't have opened with that." He slid into bed. "It's not creepy or anything like that. Honest."

"Maybe for you." I'd never conquered my fear of birds. When Zack came home from preschool with a pine cone slathered with peanut butter and birdseed, I'd hung it in the back tree, far from the house. I took it off two days later.

Michael took a deep breath. "I think the bird is my dad. When I'm running, sometimes I'm filled with a sense of peace. And then, I look up and see a bird." He shrugged "And somehow I know it's my dad. He's watching me." He reached out and squeezed my hand. "It sounds crazy, but I think he's giving me a sign."

I squeezed his hand back and nodded. But I said nothing because I didn't really believe him. He never spoke of birds again. Not until the sparrow hopped into our house ten years later. But it was more than just that tiny bird now.

For months after we lost Brendan, birds flocked to our house, covering our front lawn. They'd never done that before. Some pecked at our back door, *tap-tap-tapping*, asking to be let in. Others clung to our window screens. Three, four, sometimes five birds sat on my screens, their claws grabbing onto the mesh, staying for hours, and oh, how I wanted to believe this meant something.

I researched the meaning of birds. They meant peace and hope. Or maybe wisdom. There were so many different interpretations. A wren represented souls in paradise, but ravens and crows were omens of impending death. Birds would trick you or perhaps reveal your path to happiness. The more I researched, the more I learned they can mean anything or nothing at all. A blessing or a curse, depending on the website and your own desperate wish.

I wanted to believe. There were even moments when I did, like the day I woke up from a nap and saw three birds clinging to the screen on my bedroom window. I stared at them, and they stared back at me, and I felt something, like a tiny shard of hope piercing my grief. I wanted to scoop them up like Michael did and cradle them next to my heart.

I didn't, though. I stared at them, waiting, until they finally flew away. It was only then that I inched forward. Their claws had left marks on the screen. I scraped my finger against the rough metal, staring at the holes the birds had left behind. Somehow, it seemed like a gift.

10

Michael and I stood in the hospital hallway outside the quiet room talking to a detective. He had a kind face. *He's going to figure out what happened.* He'd told us his name, had given us his card, but I'd already forgotten it. I reached out and squeezed his hands, the same way I did to the doctor. He couldn't save our son, but this man would uncover the truth. That seemed like the most important thing right then.

"Please find out what really happened. It's not what you think," Michael said.

"Something else is going on here," I said. "I don't know what happened. But it's not this. He didn't do this."

The detective nodded and flipped open his notebook. "I will. It's my job to look at every possibility."

"Could someone have done this to him?" Michael asked. I jerked off the wall. Of course. He didn't do this to himself. Someone else came in and hurt him.

"The back door," I said. "It's usually unlocked. I have piano students who come in the back way. They don't even ring the doorbell; they just walk in. Everyone knows that. Everyone knows the back door is unlocked."

He nodded at us, but that wasn't enough for me. I needed more. I wanted him to grab on to this theory. He wrote nothing down, only paused for a moment before asking, "Did you notice any personality changes lately?"

Michael and I looked at each other, shaking our heads no.

"Did he have a fight with his girlfriend?"

"No." We couldn't help smiling at that. "He didn't have one. He was shy."

He wrote something down.

What did that mean? Should he have had a girlfriend? I should have made him go out more, meet new people. He hung out with his friends, went to the movies, but he also spent a lot of time playing video games online. I should have made him go outside more, like when he was little and I told him it was an outside day. I should have done something.

I should have known.

"Was he having trouble with any of his friends? Anyone bothering him?"

We said no. We kept saying no. We kept saying he didn't do this. And still, he asked questions. I slumped into the wall. He's not going to help us. He's already decided what happened.

"Was he depressed?" We shook our heads.

"I would have known," I whispered. I straightened. "Wait. He said, 'Yay.'" I stopped for a second, hearing his "Yay" in my mind. "I left him money for lunch with his brother, and he said, 'Yay.'" I reached for Michael's hand. "That was his last word to me. Yay."

I looked at the detective, who said nothing. Why wasn't he writing this down? No boy who shouts "Yay" to his mother would do this to himself.

He didn't write anything down.

"Was he taking drugs?"

This was so ludicrous that we both laughed, a sharp bark that echoed in the hallway. Brendan wouldn't even walk past a crowd of smokers, terrified of any poison winding its way through him. He made us all hold our breaths if we couldn't cross the street.

"This isn't Brendan. These questions," Michael said. "This isn't him."

I reached out for the detective's hand again. "He was quiet, but he's not the kid you're thinking he is. Please."

He only nodded. My hands fell away. I'm begging him. An hour before I pleaded with God and the doctors to let my son live. And now I was ready to get down on my knees and beg this detective to stop believing my son did this to himself.

What the hell is going on?

"I don't know what happened," Michael said. His words trailed off and I could feel the tremors moving through his whole body. His voice stayed strong, though. "He didn't do this. He didn't."

I fumbled for Michael's hand and held on. We're his parents. We would have known. The detective shook his head, the same way the doctor shook his head before he told us it was over. I stepped back, my hand feeling for the wall.

He wouldn't stop asking questions, just like the priest. "Was he moody? Or coming home late at night?"

He'd already determined what had happened: Brendan was a depressed teenager who no longer wanted to live. Nothing we said would change his mind. This detective asking his questions didn't know Brendan. He didn't know that the night before, Brendan had walked into the kitchen and made his famous victory nachos, layering cheese over tortilla chips, slicing salami in perfect cubes to sprinkle on top.

He didn't know that he'd knocked on my door late last night. "*Lost Girls?*" he whispered, hoping we'd watch our favorite TV show together. This wasn't a boy who was troubled or sad. This was a boy who stood in the driveway every morning on his way to the bus stop, waiting for his sister to look out her window. Once he saw her, he'd contort himself into all sorts of silly positions. He'd wave and dance and spin around. "It's his silly wave," Lizzie told me. "He gives me a different one each day."

This was the Brendan I knew. Not the one they were telling me.

"You don't know him," I told the detective. "This isn't like him. This isn't him."

He nodded, but didn't write any of that down. He kept asking his questions and we shook our heads and kept saying no.

My neighbor Patty had brought Zack to the hospital that day. When he heard the news, he slid down the wall. He howled and punched and kicked the floor. He rocked back and forth, unable to be still with his sorrow. This was Zack. He threw his whole body into everything, whether it was baseball or piano or making duct tape wallets. And now, grief.

In those early weeks, everyone worried about Zack.

"I'm not worried about Lizzie," the doctor said. "She knows how to get the feelings out. But a boy turning thirteen? That's a dangerous age."

"He needs to let it out," the guidance counselor told me and so I let him rage. He slammed his door a dozen times until the wood cracked around the edge. He jumped on the trampoline until his tears mixed with sweat. I let the anger boil through him until it bubbled over. Afterward, he'd sit next to me and talk about Brendan. He told me stories of the things they liked to do together, like waiting for the first star to appear so they could make a wish about flying pigs. He talked about walking to Valentino's for a slice of pizza that Brendan paid for and all the silly little fights they used to have.

He asked about Brendan, and I pushed through my pain and shared stories. But sometimes, Zack asked questions that were too hard to answer, the kind that pulled me out of bed and made me pace in the darkness. I answered them. I had to. Only, I did what any mother in this situation would do.

I lied.

Before that day in the hospital, my biggest lie had been when Brendan was eight and lost his stuffed animal. Eeyore was pale purple, its nap worn down. Given to him by his aunts before he was even born, Eeyore was his first friend, his pillow, his lullaby. When he was two, he stood at the bottom of the stairs each night, crying, "Night-night," slapping the steps, a demand that we carry him and Eeyore up into his crib. He'd snuggle under the covers and wave us away, eager to share dreams with his best friend.

When he was eight, I'd accidentally thrown him out. Lizzie had come home from preschool with lice and I'd bundled up all of their soft toys into a white bag that somehow found its way into the garbage.

"It's okay," he said. "I don't need him anymore."

But he came to me a few days later, tears in his eyes and I promised him I'd find his Eeyore. I found an old one listed on eBay. When it came, I loosened the stitches on its tail and rubbed away some of the fur on its ear. I told him Santa had sent it to him. I held my breath, waiting for him to examine Eeyore. Brendan questioned everything and only half believed in Santa, but he just took him in his arms and nodded.

I lied to Zack and Lizzie that day in the hospital. We were in a quiet room, the four of us and my mother. And that priest who wouldn't leave me alone. Every once in a while, he'd launch into a prayer, and my body responded without thought, crossing myself and mumbling the words. But mostly he sat in the chair and watched us. Zack turned to me and asked the question I dreaded the most, the question I didn't know how to answer.

"How did Brendan die?"

Michael said nothing. I couldn't tell the kids what the police and doctors had said. We didn't believe it, would never believe it. I looked over at the priest, but his face was blank. So I lied and told them Brendan had choked on something he was eating.

Zack picked at the rubber on his sneaker. "It was probably fruit snacks."

"Yeah," Lizzie said. "He always had them in his desk drawer."

My mother shifted in her chair. She said nothing, only nodded, but I heard what she meant. *Be strong. Stay strong for your children, the same way I did.*

I took a deep breath and inhaled her strength. This time, I didn't even look at the priest. I smiled at them, knowing exactly what to say. "He did love those fruit snacks."

Lizzie held up one hand and placed the other one over her heart. "I'll never eat them again," she swore, her eyes solemn and wide. "Not even the yellow ones. Never."

My mother nodded. "That sounds like a good idea."

Zack held up his hand too. "Me too. Never again."

"No," I said. "Never again."

Michael reached for my hand. "Never."

And the five of us moved closer, forming a circle, holding onto each other, promising to never eat fruit snacks again.

II

We discovered the truth only a few hours later. Jim's wife, Patty, came to the hospital and took the kids home with her. I didn't even worry about them; she was caring and empathetic and would know just what to do to take care of them. My brothers were waiting with my father at my house. Michael and I drove home together, my mother following us in her car.

"Don't let me get lost," she said. "I don't know the way." I'm not sure I could have found my way home either. We pulled into the driveway, followed by my mother's car Jim stood by the garage, alone. He pulled me into a hug. I thought he whispered something to me, but when I looked at him, he shook his head. He had no words.

We walked into the house and into the kitchen. My dad sat at the far end of the table. He looked so, so small, crumpled in the chair, as if broken beneath the weight of his oxygen tank. Allan sat next to him, his face in the shadows.

My brothers were so different. Jimmy took after my father with his height and fair skin and blue eyes. He was the Irish brother, with red hair and freckles, the one who had no words but stood next to me so I could lean on him and steal his strength. Allan was the opposite. We all had the same genes, but he only claimed our mother's Italian ones. He was shorter, with dark skin and hair. He was the one who teased me, who scared away boyfriends and stole my crutches when I was sixteen and had knee surgery. But he was also the brother who protected me, the one who would take care of things.

He stood up and pulled out a chair. "Why don't you sit down?" For a second I stood there, staring at the chair. Was this where Brendan sat? I couldn't tell. My father and I had moved the table the day before, testing out a new configuration for a remodel we were planning. I couldn't figure out where anyone belonged.

I couldn't sit. I shook my head. Michael sat in the chair, and I stood behind him, my fingers resting on his shaking shoulders.

"You should sit," Allan said again. There was something in his voice, something more than sorrow. *He knows something.* Michael's muscles welded together in one giant knot across his shoulders, but mine weakened, growing liquid even as the tension inside me wound tighter. I turned to Jim, but he'd wrapped an invisible wall around him. My mother kept her head down, staring at her hands. My father looked away from me. For a few moments, only the puff of his oxygen tank broke the silence.

Oh, my God. They know something.

I'd survived the last few hours by saying no. I said no when I'd seen the bruises on Brendan's neck. I said no when the detective told me they found a belt near him. When the medical examiner called us on the ride home and ruled it as a suicide. "We all know what this is," he said, and still, I shook my head no.

It was easy for me to say no. I was his mother; no one knew him better. But now, I was surrounded by family, by people who knew Brendan. The month before, we'd all crowded around this table for Brendan's fifteenth birthday. We clapped when he blew out the birthday candles on his apple pie. My father had gone to the movies with him a few weeks ago. Brendan had spent a week at Jim's house, playing miniature golf and going for ice cream with his cousins.

He and Sean played video games for hours. *Did he tell Sean secrets late at night? Does he know something?*

Allan took a deep breath. "Wait," I said. I shook my head. I'd begged the detective to find out what really happened, but that was when I didn't believe anything he said. I held onto Michael's shoulders and looked at my parents and brothers. They waited, not saying anything, the only sound that gentle puff of air. It was rhythmic, a burst of air every few seconds. I timed my own breath with his, waiting until I was ready.

I nodded. "Tell me."

Allan pointed to the open laptop in front of him. "Have you ever heard of the cinnamon challenge?"

Challenge. My legs melted. I fumbled for the chair next to Michael and sat down. We looked at each other. A challenge.

"No," I whispered, my hands covering my mouth. I bit my finger. Hard. "No."

Brendan loved a challenge. He couldn't resist a challenge.

I tried to say no again, but this time, nothing came out.

Brendan had a knack for finding the most efficient way of doing everything. He shoveled food into his mouth and played piano scales so quickly they blended into one note. When he was five and played with his plastic animals, he still wouldn't move them around the jungle mat on the floor. He stared at them while lying on the couch, imagining the giraffe eating the leaves off the tree or the rhino swimming in the river.

"It's faster that way," he said with a yawn.

He found a way to do his kindergarten homework faster. He held two pencils, one in each hand and wrote everything on the left side of the paper with his left hand, the right side with his right hand. He even used both hands to cut. His teacher had him tested to make sure he didn't have a neurological problem, but I knew it was just Brendan being as efficient as he could. There were moments when I marveled at his ingenuity, but sometimes I shook my head at his laziness.

Until he was seven and I gave him a Leap Frog, a video game to practice sight words. He no longer raced through his words. He slowed down and practiced, eager to win the challenge. He played for hours just to get to the next level.

I made charts and stickers and little prizes I bought in bulk, but it was really the challenge that motivated him. I used this weapon wisely. I created the Clean Room Challenge. The Workout Challenge. The Piano Challenge. He loved them all, but once he beat the challenge, he wanted the next one.

More, he said. *Make it harder.*

Please, Mom. I need to get to the next level.

The summer Brendan turned fifteen, he and Michael decided on the Spicy Chili Pepper Challenge. They worked their way up the levels, starting with hot buffalo wings. After each one, their fingers were stained red from the spices, coughing and hiccuping with tears streaming down their faces. Still, they kept moving up to a spicier level until we went to a Mexican restaurant and he ordered the ghost pepper chili salsa.

"It's hot," the waitress warned. "I mean, really hot. Most people can't handle it."

Brendan's eyes lit up. Challenge accepted.

A few weeks later, he asked me about another challenge. It was the beginning of August and the two of us stood in front of the stove making tacos. Brendan had perfected his scrambled eggs and the victory nachos he'd invented and now wanted to learn tacos. I showed him how to dice the onion. I threw it into hot oil. He leaned in closer to hear the sizzle, his glasses fogging from the steam. "What's next?"

"We wait a few minutes. We want the onions to brown."

"Caramelize," he said, drawing out the word. "That's where the flavor is." He stood over the pan, waiting until the onions changed color. He had patience when it came to building flavors in food.

"Now we add the meat. We want to let it brown, too."

He inhaled deeply. "Nothing better than the smell of meat." He took a wooden spoon and crumbled the ground beef, slowly stirring.

"Now we add dried onions and chili powder," I said.

"Wait a minute." He grabbed the box and read it. "That's not the directions on the box. So, that's the secret. Extra flavor." He reached into the cabinet and placed the spice bottles on the counter.

I showed him how to measure a tablespoon into the palm of his hand. He sprinkled the spices over the meat and then rinsed his hands off. Then he stopped and slowly reached back into the cabinet and grabbed a bottle of cinnamon.

I shook my head. "There's no cinnamon in this."

He nodded and leaned against the counter, the bottle still in his hand. "We should do the cinnamon challenge together." His voice was casual, as if he were talking about the latest movie.

I frowned. "What's that?"

"You swallow a teaspoon of cinnamon. The trick is to do it without drinking any water."

I laughed and shook my head. I couldn't even handle the hot wing challenge he and Michael had done. I didn't even smell their ghost pepper salsa weeks before.

Brendan waited. After a few moments, he put the bottle away and went back to stealing little bits of browned meat.

I have so many moments, little slices of time I wish I could freeze and rewind and do again. But if I could only choose one moment, it's that day we stood in the kitchen making tacos.

Instead of sprinkling dried onions onto the meat, I wish I'd asked him to tell me more. I wish I'd shut off the stove, and together we'd sat at the table while we watched YouTube videos. We'd done that a few weeks before when he'd shown me some silly video of a man chasing someone with a spoon.

Would I have laughed at the cinnamon challenge like I had at the absurd image of a man running from a spoon? Maybe. I might have thought it was stupid and walked away. Or maybe I would have realized the kids doing the challenge weren't just coughing. That the cinnamon dried out their throats and made them choke and gasp for air. I might have noticed their grins when the rush of oxygen finally flooded their brains and gave them a high they thought was safe.

I know for sure if I sat with him and watched, I would have seen the videos on the right. The ones that pop up, suggesting the next video to watch. Those videos weren't about cinnamon. They were about the next level, the next challenge.

The choking challenge.

If I'd seen those videos, I would have told him about the dangers. I would have grabbed his laptop and researched the choking game, the way I did after he'd died. I would have learned that sometimes, boys played this game alone. They chose this game because the lack of oxygen gave them a high that didn't involve drugs. They thought it was safe.

I would have discovered dozens of videos of kids taking the challenge. A stupid party game, with everyone laughing when a boy fell to the ground after wrapping a scarf around his neck. I would have seen this boy pop back up, holding his thumb high when the oxygen rushed to his brain. I would have heard the crowd of people clapping and cheering, making it seem like a harmless playground game.

I would have seen all of this. And then, I would have told him it was dangerous. I would have told him that sometimes when you pass out, your heart stops for a few seconds. And in rare cases, even if it's the very first time you ever try this stupid game, your brain doesn't know how to tell your heart to beat again. I would have told him this. And, oh, this I know: he would have listened.

He had no fear, not when he thought something was safe. He rode a roller coaster by himself when he was eight. When he was thirteen, he rappelled down an eighty-foot mountain after the guide showed him the safety ropes. He rushed to the sink every afternoon, coming off the bus, to wash his hands because science made him wary of germs. He'd scan every food package, checking for trans-fat. Just a few words from me that day, and he would have listened.

His cheeks would have flushed. "I got it, I got it," he would have said, nodding his head until his hair fell into his eyes. I wouldn't have had to warn him more than once. Just a few words from me, and he never would have tried it.

That's not what happened, no matter how many times I replay that day in my head.

Instead, I laughed over the silly idea of swallowing cinnamon and then reached for the water and showed him how to pour it over the meat without splattering. We stood there, watching the meat bubble and simmer.

I didn't know.

I didn't know that, a week before his first day of high school, Brendan would watch one of those videos. He'd see that next level.

More, Mom. I need the next level.

More.

He'd hear them laughing and think it was just a game. Something silly. Something safe.

I said nothing that day when we stood in the kitchen, making tacos together.

And a few weeks later, on that last Tuesday in August, Brendan tried his final challenge.

12

I once believed that I could make my sister dream about my stories. I was ten; she was eight and sick with yet another cold. We sat in our beds, propped up by pillows, our pink chenille bedspreads folded by our feet. We each had a small, white canopy hanging from the ceiling. My father had soaked long strips of wood in the bathtub, waiting until they were pliable enough to be shaped into half-moons and then covered in a curtain of white.

Elizabeth's bed was filled with stuffed animals, her arm wrapped around her favorite dog with floppy brown ears. She laughed at my stories and always wanted more. I whispered one about a princess and rainbows. Then I got out of bed and grabbed her pillow.

"The secret is the pillow," I said. I hugged it, squeezing hard as I hummed a melody from Mozart into it, a song my piano teacher had taught me. Then I sang its melody, making up lyrics, something silly about a princess riding rainbows.

She giggled. "But what if I wake up in the middle of the night scared?"

"That's when you change the channel. The pillow is like a TV. There's always a different story." I took her pillow and flipped it over, this time humming Beethoven into it. I sang a story about the Brady Bunch meeting the Partridge Family. She fell back on her pillow and smiled. I sang a lullaby until she fell asleep, my songs seeping inside her dreams. Even as she grew older, I'd spin stories for her, weaving in the sounds of Happy the Hamster cycling on his wheel.

I don't remember having my own dreams.

Michael dreamt of Brendan the first morning after we'd lost him. The sun was just beginning to rise. I'd only slept for an hour or two. I was in the den, watching yellow and orange bleed into the sky, shocked that the world wasn't forever cloaked in darkness. I heard Michael cry out and the scratch of Snowy's toenails as they ran down the stairs.

"He came to me," he said. "I felt him. It was like he jumped inside me." His voice was filled with awe, the same wonder he'd have in a few hours when he'd cradle the bird in his hand. "Snowy felt it too. She started barking just as he came to me. She was so happy. I know she felt him."

He took my hands, as if I could feel our son too, but I felt nothing, only the cold trembling of his fingers.

He dreamt of Brendan often. Quick snippets that he could piece together, like a quilt warming him even on the coldest days. He saw Brendan in the car reaching for the nuts Michael always kept on the front seat. "Who keeps nuts in their car?" Brendan asked, his hands stretched out wide. He saw the two of them riding bikes on the trail, the wind blowing Brendan's hair into his eyes as they pedaled faster, trying to beat their old record. My favorite dream that Michael shared was Brendan clutching his stomach, doubled over with laughter, his eyes tearing as he howled. They weren't really dreams but memories of the Brendan we knew.

Oh, how I wanted to hear his laugh, to watch him shake with joy. I wanted to hear his high-pitched giggle or that deep belly laugh that made everyone in the room laugh with him. Even the sarcastic snort that once annoyed me. I wanted to hear it all.

I searched for him in my dreams. I'd take anything, even a shape-less dream with just a hint of his presence. I tried everything, even whispered stories into my pillow and hummed a melody, trying to lure him into my dreams. I couldn't find him.

And yet, somehow, I knew my dreams weren't empty. I woke up, my hands tingling as if I'd held something. I couldn't see anything in the shadows of my dreams, but there was something there. I could almost feel it beneath my hands, something that pulsed with meaning.

It was like a golden liquid flowing inside me, warming me and filling me with a tiny trickle of light.

13

I was fourteen when a priest came to our house for the first time. I didn't watch him walk the short distance from the church to our house, but in my mind I pictured two altar boys dressed in black-and-white robes, marching down the block, holding golden poles topped with burning incense, the priest behind them dressed like a king, bathed in a cloud of smoke. The altar boys stayed on our front steps while the priest entered our house, reaching into his chalice of holy water and sprinkling the air.

I didn't go downstairs. I hid on the landing, my cheek pressed against the wallpaper, straining to hear him speak to my mother. There were no altar boys. He came alone, dressed in black pants and shirt. He sat down in the kitchen with my mother while I huddled alone on the stairs, waiting for explanations.

I'd offered God everything I had. I listened to my teachers and saved every prayer and good deed. They called it a spiritual bank, and I'd saved for years. I already knew about banks from my father who worked on Wall Street. A banker's bank, he called it. In the top drawer of his dresser, he had a piece of paper with four columns, one for each of us kids. It was his very own Daddy Bank. Each week, we handed over part of our allowance and sat down with him in his study and learned how interest made money grow on its own.

I was determined to make my spiritual bank as rich as possible. I made a list of extra chores and good deeds I could do, but it was never enough. I'd organize the comic books in the den, but then erase that checkmark when I teased Allan by calling him Grape or snuck an Almond Joy from my sister's Halloween pumpkin.

I added extra prayers at night to grow my account. I'd fall asleep with a rosary wrapped around my fingers, waking up in the morning with an imprint of a cross etched into my palm. I traced the cross with my finger and wondered how much this added to my account.

I hid my statement on a piece of paper hidden inside the pages of my Bible. Jimmy and Allan had already found my diary hidden beneath my grandmother's sewing machine, but I knew they'd never look in my Bible.

Like the bank in my father's drawer, I never squandered my spiritual money. I didn't ask God to help me with my science project on leukemia or make me the fastest swimmer on the block. For years I let my bank grow. I didn't even ask for help when my sister started going to the hospital for chemotherapy. Not when her hair started falling out or when she could no longer go to school and Mrs. Green came to our house to tutor her.

I was convinced he would save Elizabeth, that he was stronger than cancer could ever be. I saved and saved, until I was fourteen and had more than enough in my spiritual bank to bargain with God. I believed in the power of that bank. I believed in God. I swear I did everything right.

But he didn't save my sister, and a week later, I sat on the stairs trying to understand why. I was empty inside and only wanted God to fill me up again. I didn't know how to do it on my own, and I thought this priest would have the answers.

His voice was too low to make out what he was saying. I sat on the stairs, lulled by the cadence of his words. They seemed heavy with meaning, like a sermon—no, like a song—and I rocked to its rhythm, trying to ease the ache inside me. I jumped up at the scrape of chairs and then the footsteps in the hallway. I raised up on my toes, as if I were about to sing the Amen and feel that sense of peace fill me.

Hidden in the shadows, I strained toward him. *Make me understand.*

I knew the science of cancer and death, but I believed in faith. I never once questioned the rules of God or his power. I only wanted to understand.

Please, make me understand.

I held my breath, waiting for answers.

"Now, remember," he said to my mother as they moved toward the front door. "This is God's will." He reached for the doorknob. "I know it hurts, but this is God's will."

I shivered as his words echoed inside me. I gripped the banister with shaking hands and climbed back up the stairs to my room, trying to understand his words. I'd offered God everything. He'd taken it all, every last drop of me until I was hollow inside. Then he'd taken my sister and left me with nothing. I had waited in the dark to hear the priest offer God's power, to find a way to make me understand, but he offered me nothing but empty words. He said them as an afterthought. He'd been on his way out the door when he turned and tossed over his shoulder the words that pierced me.

This is God's will.

What kind of God wants us to feel this pain, to put us through this heartache?

I'd believed everything they told me since I was a little girl. Each week, I stood on my toes, straining to be closer to God. I sang the Amen. I felt it flow through me. I believed. Until that priest turned and spoke of God's will. His words ripped the Amen out of me, leaving me dry and barren.

I pulled the blind in my window and watched him walk away. My imagination played no tricks here. There were no altar boys, no robes that reeked of power. He walked down the empty street, alone, just a man dressed in black.

I still went to church with my parents. My body went through the motions, a reflex of standing, kneeling, and crossing myself. But I no longer believed in God's power. I no longer believed in a God that was with me at all times.

I didn't say the prayers at church or even whisper them late at night in the room I no longer shared with my sister. I asked him for nothing. I didn't ask for help to pass my calculus test. I didn't ask him to take away the pain of my knee surgery or help when my doctor told me he doubted I'd ever get pregnant.

I never thanked God, either. Not when I met Michael or when we bought our house or had our children. I couldn't believe in a God that gave me happiness because then I would need to believe in a God that inflicted pain.

Over the years, a coldness filled the emptiness inside me until I was numb. When the kids were young, I took them to church. But I resented the rules of religion, and we rarely went. I never prayed to God or asked him for anything again, not until that day in the hospital, when I stood over my fifteen-year-old son and asked God to save him. I didn't ask that day. I begged. Over and over.

Please, God. Don't let my son die.

14

Allan and Becky were hosting the funeral lunch. I spent far too long picking out dishes that Brendan would have loved. Chicken parmigiana with a thick layer of melted mozzarella cheese. Meatballs studded with garlic and little flecks of parsley. And steak tips swimming in a thick brown sauce. Allan kept track of it all. I would have been lost without him. As soon as I finished one item on our checklist, another was placed in front of me, like a moving assembly line of grief.

I was grateful for these pockets of time that pulled me away just a bit from my pain. I focused on each task, losing myself in meaningless details like the quality of the lining in the casket and deciding between penne vodka and chicken parmigiana. I spent the most time on the wording of the funeral card. At the bottom of the card, I added something Brendan used to say as a toddler. *Lights out, glasses off, head on pillow.* For years, he said it every night when Michael put him to bed. He wanted him to lay down next to him, his head sharing the same pillow, knowing his daddy would fall asleep and stay with him for hours. All he wanted was time.

I shook my head when it came to planning the actual service. We still belonged to the Catholic church around the corner, the one where all three kids were baptized, but it was years since we had been there. I refused to even speak to a Catholic priest. I was afraid he might believe the original police report and try to convince me of God's judgment.

Allan called the minister from a local church. I'd visited the United Presbyterian Church only once before. The minister agreed to come to our house. I refused to go there. I didn't want to walk into his church and sit on one of the wooden pews while he tried to promise me God's comfort. Or speak of God's will the way the priest had to my mother so many years before.

The Reverend Rick came to our house. He wore sandals and round glasses too small for his face, just an ordinary man. "Call me Rev. Rick," he said when we shook hands. It had been thirty years since a holy man had walked down the block into my childhood home, but this time, I had no expectations. I wasn't crouched on the stairs, waiting for healing words to flow over me like some spiritual balm.

As soon as I saw him, I wanted him gone. He carried something in his hand. I was afraid it was a Bible. I didn't want him opening it up, pointing to a passage and cherry-picking words he was certain would heal me. But mostly, I didn't want him asking me how Brendan died. We knew the truth now, but the word *suicide* still rang inside my head, pushing away any other thoughts. I was afraid he wouldn't believe us, afraid he'd open to the Bible and point to a passage meant to condemn.

It was that same feeling I had the night Brendan died when a line of cars rolled by our house. Neighbors nodded at us as they went by, their hands on their hearts, offering us wordless comfort. Some took the time to get out of the car and hug us. Others left coffee cakes on our front steps. But in each offering, I felt the weight of their own fears. *Could this happen to my child?* It was an unthinkable thought, an easy one to push away. *This wouldn't have happened to my child.*

She must have done something wrong. I felt their judgment and knew they were right; this was my fault, and no baked good could ever make up for it.

Michael showed Rev. Rick into the piano room, and the three of us stood around the table in front of the bookcases, pretending this was a social visit. Before we could sit, Michael launched into his bird story. He told it the way he always did, bouncing on his toes while he went through the motions. My cheeks burned red, and I tried giving him a look to make him stop, but Michael acted out the whole story. I watched Rev. Rick's face when Michael's voice filled with wonder. He listened but showed no emotion.

"And that's when I knew the bird was Brendan," Michael said, his hands clasped over his heart. He sighed, and I couldn't stop my own silent sigh from joining his.

Rev. Rick nodded, "Well," he said with a shrug, "stranger things have happened."

I knew exactly what that meant. It was code for *I think you're crazy, but I'm going to humor the grieving parents.* I wanted him gone, but he sat down. He looked as if he were about to start a prayer, but he took a deep breath and then nodded again. "It's okay to be angry with God."

I almost laughed. I had no problems being angry with God. I'd been angry with God since I was a teenager. And now fury burned through me with every breath. I turned to leave the room, but he pointed to our chairs. "Why don't you tell me what happened? How did your son die?"

We sat down, and Michael took a deep breath. This wasn't the story he wanted to tell. This one wasn't filled with hope. Under the table, I slipped off my shoes, rocking them back and forth with my feet. Again, I watched Rev. Rick's face when Michael spoke of what the police initially believed. How the medical examiner had issued a death certificate within the first hour, listing the cause of death as suicide. None of us had believed it. None of his friends or teachers believed it either.

I'd spent hours researching the choking game; we knew what really happened, but I couldn't erase the word *suicide* etched deep inside me. I couldn't even whisper the word. I winced when Michael said it. When he got to the part about the choking game, Rev. Rick raised his eyebrows again.

Does he believe us? Does he think we're bad parents?

I searched his face for signs of judgment, but it was neutral, a mask he slipped on to soothe. I wiggled on my shoes again, ready to flee the room, but then he leaned back. "Tell me about Brendan."

He didn't open his notebook to take notes. He rested his hands on his stomach and waited, as if he really wanted to know Brendan.

This was his job; he needed to talk about him at the funeral. But he was the first stranger to really ask us about our son. He wasn't a case number to solve. He wasn't the police asking us about drug use and depression. They didn't want to talk about his marathon Monopoly games and the way he'd risk it all to buy Park Place. They didn't want to hear about his hugs and the way he counted to three under his breath to make sure they were long enough. But the Rev? He waited for us to tell stories about Brendan.

We couldn't stop talking about him. We talked about how smart he was and the way he snorted and giggled if you tickled him under his chin. We talked about how loyal he was to Snowy. One weekend, we looked after a friend's dog, and he refused to even look at the other dog.

"I don't want Snowy to feel bad," he said as he sidestepped past the other dog, his gaze glued to his own dog.

Most of our stories involved his obsession with food.

"He loved food," I said. "After 'Mama' and 'Dada,' 'more' was his first word. He'd sit in his high chair banging on the tray. 'More,' he'd say." I drew the word out into three syllables, just like Brendan used to. "When he was two, my father brought over a leftover prime rib. Brendan's eyes grew wide when my father unwrapped the foil. He shoved his face into it and started chewing."

"After that, he was obsessed with meat," Michael said. "He had a special belly dance he'd do when he was full." We both smiled as we pictured him shimmying across the kitchen, hoping to make room for more meat.

"He even asked for a crockpot when he turned thirteen," I said. "We already had one, but he wanted his own in his room. So he could always be surrounded by the smell of meat. He wanted it to be his alarm clock because he could never sleep through the smell of roasting meat."

Rev. Rick laughed, and Michael and I smiled at each other. Some of my panic eased as stories flooded me. Two nights ago, that first night, icy shock had tricked me into believing I was strong. But it had also robbed me of memories. I'd panicked when I couldn't remember anything about Monday, our last day with Brendan.

"What was his last meal?" I asked Lizzie.

"What about his favorite TV shows?" I asked Zack.

I grabbed a notebook and started writing things down, terrified I'd lose the memories as well as my son. *Lemon Chicken. The TV show* Eureka *about a town filled with scientific geniuses.*

Talking about him made me feel as if I'd gotten back a small part of Brendan. It made it easier when Rev. Rick opened his notebook and started talking about the funeral service, the music, the reading Zack would do.

"Since your families are Jewish and Catholic, I'll print a version of the Our Father in the bulletin."

I could almost hear Brendan laughing at the idea of a Presbyterian church filled with Jews and Catholics. When we finished discussing the details, Rev. Rick hesitated, his hand resting on his closed notebook.

"People like to talk about God in situations like these. The death of a child—" He shook his head. "It's unimaginable. Some people are even going to say this is God's will. But they're wrong. This isn't what God wants."

He said all the right words. He made me remember Brendan's joy in food and the way his laughter filled my heart. Still, I wanted him gone.

15

Rev. Rick stood up to leave, but first, he walked over to my piano and played a few notes. "I come from a family of musicians. Someday, you'll have to play for me."

I nodded, pretending my whole body wasn't suddenly filled with fear. Michael walked him to his car, and I stood over my piano staring down at the keys. I bent over my piano, searching for Brendan's fingerprints. He hadn't played the piano in over a year, had quit when he was fourteen, but I rarely polished the sides of my piano. His prints were scattered here, mixed in with mine.

I sat down on the bench and played a note in the middle of the piano. D. It was the note I always taught first. It's the easiest to find because even the youngest can see that the black keys are in groups of two or three. The D was in between the two black keys. I played it again. There, in that one note, was the beginning of a story, one that began when Brendan was three. I'd put Zack down for a nap, and he'd climb onto the bench next to me.

He giggled and curled his hands into a loose fist and knocked on the groups of two black keys. He moved up the piano, counting each group. One, two, three, until he got to seven. He smiled. "That's my favorite number." He leaned forward and whispered, "It's the one Daddy always chooses when we play the guessing game. It's always seven."

"Which group is your favorite?" I asked.

"That's easy," he said and ran to the lowest one and smacked it. "It sounds like a T-Rex growling."

He crouched low and stomped all over the room. He had dinosaurs sleeping on his pillow and lined up on the couch. He had dinosaur sneakers on, the kind that lit up when he ran. He giggled and ran over to the piano and knocked again on the black keys.

"It's the black keys that tell us how to find the other notes," I told him. "They're like a map that shows you the way. Watch." He leaned in until his nose almost touched the black keys. I pressed the two black keys, first together and then one note at a time.

"Fiddle fiddle, D's in the middle," I chanted, sliding my finger into the white key between the two black keys. "That's the D."

Brendan copied me, pressing the two black keys and then sliding his pointer finger to the D. "I know where the Ds are." He smiled and played all seven of them, high and low.

"Let me tell you a secret," I whispered. He leaned closer. "Even without seeing them, you can still find the D. You don't need your eyes. You can feel for the two black key groups."

His eyes widened, but then he closed them and reached out, his fingers fumbling for the black keys and then sliding into the D. He laughed, his eyes still closed and found another one and then another.

That night, he tiptoed into the piano room, closed his eyes, and made up songs of dinosaurs dancing in the dark. "I don't need to see," he whispered. "It's like magic."

Now, alone in my piano room, I played the D, each one telling me a story of Brendan throughout the years. I closed my eyes and felt for them, using the pedal to sustain the notes. I kept playing Ds, letting them ring. I swayed a bit, moving toward the sound, like a magnet pulling me in. The notes layered on top of each other. They moved around me until I was wrapped in sound and story. *Brendan's first piano lesson. His first recital at the church around the corner.*

I moved faster, reaching for Ds both high and low. I rocked back and forth on the bench, my arms wide. The notes moved closer, tightening around me. I could barely breathe.

The first time he used the pedals.

The prizes he won for a piano challenge. Oh, how he loved his challenges.

I played only bass notes now, and the sound turned dark and muddy. They felt like danger. *The police searching his room.* I struggled for breath, and still I played that D over and over, each one layering on top of the other. The bench lifted off its back legs as I moved faster. I grew dizzy, spots flashing before my eyes. My breath burst out of me, and still I played that D.

The day he stood in my kitchen, asking about the cinnamon challenge.

I bared my teeth like an animal, wild and feral, but I couldn't stop. I rocked faster, hitting that D, feeling the music build until it felt like it would break me.

His final challenge.

I slammed my arm down one last time, my middle finger hitting the lowest D. I cut off the pedal and the dampers muffled the strings. There was silence now, but still his story screamed inside me.

I looked up and saw Michael leaning on the doorframe, his eyebrows raised.

I shook my head, answering his unspoken question. I stood up and pushed the bench under the piano. I closed the lid.

"I'll never play again."

16

It was music that made me fall in love with Michael when I was only twenty-one. We met when Allan kept dragging Michael home with him after nights of drinking. In the morning, Michael would shuffle into the hallway, his eyes red and puffy from sleeping in his contacts, his nose dripping from his allergies to our cat.

"Him?" my parents asked, their eyes wide, when we started dating a few months later. In those early days when he was just Allan's friend, they'd seen the worst of him. I had too. His wild hair and swollen eyes and croaky voice. But his laughter changed my mind. I fell for his crooked smile and his quirky humor and oh, the fat orange stripe he'd painted around the walls of his bedroom so that he was always surrounded by laughter.

He took me to a record store after we'd been dating for about a month. I'd been in only one record store before, with my piano teacher. Mrs. Bain and I had browsed through Beethoven and Bach. I was a classically trained pianist and rarely listened to popular music. Allan hated me banging on the piano and insisted on no music—not even rock music—playing in the car. I didn't even know who The Beatles were when John Lennon died.

Michael's record store was dark and smelled of smoke and incense. I wandered the maze of cardboard boxes, flipping through records, most of the bands unfamiliar to me. Michael kept finding me, each time holding up another favorite record, his fingers brushing against the cover as if he were introducing me to an old friend.

"Check this one out," he said. REM. I shrugged.

"No? What about this one?" I shook my head. His mouth opened wide. "Not even The Who?"

For hours, we walked around the store, and I entered a different world of music. I knew Barbra Streisand and Neil Diamond from my mother's 8-track collection. In the basement we had a real jukebox, stuffed with records from the 1950s. On Sundays, my father played German music that mostly celebrated the art of drinking. My sister and I used to swing our glasses of milk and chug it down in 3/4 time.

But rock music was new to me; Mrs. Bain considered even Billy Joel's "Piano Man" too modern. After browsing for a while, we moved into the section of CD players. It was a fairly new technology, one that allowed you to skip to any track you wanted. Michael had bought his first CD player a week before and was eager to add to his collection.

He slipped on headphones and closed his eyes, rocking to the music. He had no sense of rhythm and played no instrument. He couldn't even hum a melody in tune. None of that mattered because he smiled and swayed and felt the music inside him, just like I did.

His soft smile seduced me, his rocking back and forth on his heels, and oh, the way he kept his eyes closed, feeling the music grow within. After a while, he opened his eyes. He smiled at me and tugged on my arm, pulling me closer. The music spilled out from his headphones, U2's "With or Without You." He wrapped his arms around me, and I felt the music echo inside my chest. He twisted half the headphone around and pressed it to my ear, sharing his song with me.

I knew I'd marry Michael a few months after we'd visited the record store. I stood in his bedroom with the orange stripe and green carpet and watched him sit on his bed and put on shoes. We were getting ready to go to the movies. He held one shoe in his hand, ready to slip his foot inside when he stopped. "What am I doing? We need music for this."

He jumped up and bent over the pile of CDs stacked on his wicker dresser. He shuffled through them, reading the song titles on the back. I looked at my watch. "The movie starts in fifteen minutes," I said.

He nodded, his head still bent over the CDs. "That gives me just enough time to find the perfect song for putting on my shoes."

I no longer remember which song he chose. Maybe it was Paul Simon's "Diamonds on the Soles of her Shoes." Or Elvis Costello's "Shoes without Heels." He might have even reached for his collection of cassettes or the dozens of mixtapes he'd made. We were late to the movies that night. We missed all the coming attractions and the start of the show, but I didn't mind because he'd taken the time to find the perfect song for putting on shoes.

We created soundtracks for every stage in our life. I didn't care where we got married or whether I carried tulips or roses, but we spent weeks crafting the perfect playlist for our wedding. We bought CDs for lazy Sunday afternoons and for walks in the park and even for those rare times after a fight. Together, we listened to songs and created playlists.

When we moved to New Jersey, I finally bought a piano of my own. Michael rarely gave me flowers. Instead, he brought home crumpled slips of paper, song titles written on them. "You have to learn this one," he said. I smoothed out the paper. Duran Duran's "Ordinary World." I learned the song, and he stretched out on the floor of the piano room. There was no furniture; we'd spent all our money on the baby grand, but it didn't matter. We had music.

"Please learn a Beatles song next," he begged.

When I was pregnant with Brendan, I didn't bother with a birth plan. I didn't really care about packing the right slippers for the hospital, but I made sure I brought three different CDs. I brought five when I was in labor with Zack. The iPod made it so much easier by the time Lizzie was a baby. We could move songs around easily. Still, we chose each song carefully, as if we were crafting a mixtape on cassette instead of a playlist that could easily be changed with a few clicks. We made soundtracks for our lives together.

We never once imagined we'd make a soundtrack the night our son died.

17

We'd closed Brendan's bedroom door that first night. I couldn't open it, not even when Snowy scratched at his door for hours, begging for him. That was their game. Each night, Brendan would call for Snowy to come into his room, but she'd turn her head and walk away. An hour or so later, she'd whimper outside his door. I'm not sure if he heard her in his sleep or if he waited for her call, but each night he got up and carried her into his bed.

Now, the morning of his wake, I pushed open his door slowly. I jerked my gaze away from his desk, which was bare, except for the dusty outline of what should have been there. The police had taken his computer and his phone. I rummaged through his dresser drawers and then his closet. I didn't lift up his mattress like the police had, but then, I wasn't searching for evidence.

"Fill the room," the funeral director had said the day before, his arm sweeping across the space where we'd hold the wake. He was young and carried a clipboard. He kept glancing at it, a reminder of what needed to be done.

Michael and I scanned the reception room. It was large with windows that let in light and rows of chairs set up in the middle. We turned and looked at all four walls, nodding as if it mattered where we said goodbye to our son.

"Here's where we'll set up the poster of pictures," the funeral director continued. "And over here, a banner celebrating his life. The table, the window ledges, that's all for you to fill."

"With what?" I asked, wishing I'd brought a notebook. I wanted to take notes, wanted to make sure I did everything right.

"Parents like to bring in things of their child. Anything that shows their personality. Books. Toys. Trophies."

I nodded as if I knew what he meant, but I stood now in Brendan's empty room, searching. Brendan didn't have a collection of sneakers like Zack. He didn't have a shelf with a row of trophies and ribbons like Lizzie. I couldn't even bring his computer or phone, the two things he'd cherished the most.

Michael walked into Brendan's room. "There's nothing," I said.

The week before, Brendan had cleaned out his room. He'd filled black bags with notebooks and childhood toys and pizza boxes. "I want a fresh start for high school," he'd said.

I held up my empty hands. "There's nothing here."

Michael walked to his closet. "It seems so bare."

"Only one," I whispered.

Michael reached out and touched a T-shirt. "Only one."

When Brendan was a toddler, I'd bought a small mountain of Christmas gifts for him. After opening his first box, he pushed them all away and sat down to play with his Elmo. "Only one," he cried when I placed another present in his lap. "Only one."

Even as a teen, he asked for only one gift from us. He had one pair of shoes. One jacket. He limited his shirts and pants. One time during a growth spurt, he asked for new clothes, and I rushed to Target and bought him an armful of new clothes, unaware that Michael was doing the same thing. We overwhelmed him. He shook his head at the pile of clothes. "Nope. I only need five shirts. And three pairs of jeans. I can't wear more than one at a time." He'd counted them out and then shoved the rest back into their bags to be returned.

Michael and I stared at his closet now, searching for something, anything that showed his personality.

"What about his Eeyore?" Michael asked.

I reached inside his closet for his Eeyore, the one Brendan never knew I'd replaced. He'd kept only two things when he cleaned out his room the week before—the box filled with rocks his grandmother had given him and his Eeyore. The rocks because he loved holding chipped pieces of earth millions of years old, and Eeyore for his dreams to come.

"Someday I'll give him to my child," he'd said, surprising me since he rarely spoke of his future dreams. I almost ran over and hugged him, but he was fifteen, and I knew enough to resist. When I'd placed Eeyore on the shelf that day, I smiled as I pictured the future, when I'd take him down and place him in the arms of Brendan's baby. I never imagined I'd reach for Eeyore a week later.

I hugged him to my chest, breathing in the faint smells of pizza and gummy worms. "Yes, that's good. But we need something of him now. Not just as a baby."

We stayed in his room for a long time, searching for something that seemed like him. In the end, we only brought Eeyore and the box to his favorite video game, The World of Warcraft. The game was played online, so the box held no disk. It echoed the emptiness inside us.

The day of the wake, Allan and I spent an hour in the basement, huddled over the computer as we researched, trying to choose an article that explained everything. Some articles called it The Choking Challenge. Others called it The Pass Out Game, or The Fainting Challenge.

Oh, my God. The Fainting Game. I looked up as Patty walked into the room. She kept trying to get me to eat, but I couldn't. She handed me an iced tea. "You need to drink," she murmured. She always seemed to know when my throat dried out.

"It's my fault," I whispered. "I'm the one who told Brendan that I played it once when I was little. I made it seem like a game."

It became popular for a few days when I was in fourth grade. I tried it once, panting until I grew breathless. My friend pressed against my chest. I pretended to faint. It was just a stupid game. We moved on to tag and kickball. I'd forgotten all about it until the summer before when I mentioned it to Brendan.

I said it in passing, perhaps over something someone else said. I don't remember. Maybe my tone was reminiscent, as if I were laughing over a prank, like the time we wound an entire case of toilet paper through the trees of the house on the corner. Maybe I smiled and talked about it as if it were a rite of passage, something all kids go through like setting up a lemonade stand while we watched the boys play street hockey.

Did I tell him about the dangers of trying to make yourself pass out? I don't remember. The moment had been so small to me, the memory scattering like leaves in the wind.

But not for him. Not for him.

I spent a long time that morning, hunting for the perfect label, trying to find one that didn't make me want to throw up. Finally, Allan shook his head and touched my arm. "I don't think it matters what it's called."

He was right, but I wasn't really searching for the perfect name for this stupid game. I didn't want any of the blame to fall on Brendan. I was trying to find something that would explain why he did it. I didn't want people whispering at his wake. *Why would he do this? How could he play such a dangerous game? What kind of child plays this stupid game?* But mostly, I didn't want to hear the rumors.

Rumors had swirled the moment police lights flashed on our block. Before the doctor shook his head at us the final time, before the detective pulled us out into the hallway, rumors had sprung to life. They spread through the web of social media, weaving lies and speculations, probably unaware that I was reading every word.

Strangers searched for answers. Someone whispered the word bullied and people nodded, saying yes, that's it. *He was a quiet child. Only had a few friends. He must have been bullied.*

Strangers took up the word *bullied* like a war cry, waving it like a banner within hours of his death. Before we even arrived home that day from the hospital, a Facebook page on bullying had already been created and dedicated to Brendan.

At the funeral home, instead of filling the reception room with Brendan's possessions, I handed out flyers. Surrounded by a giant picture of Brendan holding a crab and flower displays he wouldn't have wanted, I placed the stack of flyers on the little table, right next to the registry. I kept a few to hold in my hand. Then I stood in the front of the room, waiting as a line of people snaked out the door. One by one, they grabbed hold of my hand or hugged me, not letting go even when I tried to step back. Bruises from their hugs would bloom the next day, shadowing my ribs and shoulders.

His friends, neighbors, and teachers wanted to offer me comfort. I ended the hugs early, handing them the flyer, offering them evidence. I didn't want them thinking there was something wrong with Brendan. I wanted them to know this was all a horrible accident. "Boys like to do this alone," I told his music teacher, the one who'd tried to convince him to play the piano for the school's talent show.

"They're afraid of drugs and so they try this instead. They think it'll give them a high," I told the family who babysat him so many years ago. "A high they think is safe."

"The police make mistakes in these cases," I told his former Boy Scout leader. He'd looked at me for too long. He must have heard the rumors. "This isn't Brendan."

I searched their eyes for signs of skepticism. I shoved flyers and facts at people until my brother Jim walked toward the casket, carrying a cardboard case from White Castle. The box was empty; Brendan's cousins had just eaten the hamburgers. Jim placed it on the wooden table next to the casket, next to Eeyore and the empty video game box.

I hated looking at it. I was supposed to fill this room with Brendan, and all we had were empty boxes. The lingering smell of onions and steamed beef turned my stomach. I wanted it gone. And yet, Brendan would have loved seeing that box. He could eat a dozen of the tiny burgers. He was furious the time Michael teased him by driving through White Castle and only ordering one hamburger each.

I looked at the corner of the room, at Zack and Lizzie huddled with their cousins. Brendan loved sharing food with them. He scrambled eggs for his cousins AJ and Sean late at night. He saved his money to take Lizzie to Subway or Zack to Valentino's for pizza. The summer before, he'd run to us when he discovered Sean had never tasted pastrami.

"Can you believe he's never tried pastrami? We have to take him to Katz's Deli," he said. "Next week. Maybe even tomorrow. I can't take the chance he'll try pastrami without me." He tilted his head and smiled, rubbing his hands together in anticipation. "I want to see his face when he bites into that sandwich. Sean's going to love it. I can't wait."

He pestered Michael until he took them into the city a few days later. Brendan came home and rushed to tell me every detail. "I knew Sean was going to love it, Mom. He closed his eyes for each bite. And he kept smiling the most perfect smile." He started making a list of foods he wanted Sean to try—schnitzel and matzoh ball soup and escargot.

This. This is what I want to tell people about Brendan.

I didn't want to talk about the way he died. I wanted to talk about the way he lived. I crumpled the flyers in my hand. I asked Allan to take away the ones at the front of the room.

Instead of facts, I began sharing stories. "He made videos and PowerPoint presentations trying to convince us to order in pizza," I told his best friends Tim, Tony, and Alex. They had their own stories of how much Brendan loved food.

"When he went on a camping trip, he handed me a note," I said to his science teacher, the one who'd inspired him to buy his lizard. "I thought it would be about him missing me or something." I smiled. "It was a list of restaurants, all the places I couldn't go to while he was gone."

I'd offered to bring him home takeout, but he shook his head. "Absolutely not. You can't go there without me. I have to be there."

We never filled that room with Brendan's things, nothing beyond his Eeyore and two empty boxes. There was no collection of trophies or toys. But as I shared stories with those who knew him, I realized that Brendan did have a collection, only his was filled with experiences. He loved food, but even more than that, he loved sharing food with those he loved. That was his treasure.

I took home that empty White Castle box and placed it in his closet, a reminder of the memories that Brendan had cherished.

I'd planned on slipping Eeyore into his casket the next morning. I liked the idea of Brendan holding him forever, but when it was time to close the casket, I couldn't do it. I held Eeyore under my arm, squeezing him against my body. I carried him back into our house and placed him on my pillow.

I couldn't let go of my son's dreams.

18

I don't tell anyone, but I have my own bird story. The morning of the funeral, I went down into the basement to print out photographs. I walked past the four pianos I used for teaching and stood at my desk, watching an image of Brendan holding a crab appear line by line in the printer.

I heard a gentle knock. I looked around, but couldn't find where it was coming from. I grabbed the picture of Brendan and ignored the sound, used to all the weird basement noises. None of my kids would sleep in the basement when they were little, frightened by the trickle of water through the pipes or the creak of footsteps above them.

I moved toward the stairs but then stopped, hearing the sound again. The tapping came from the back door, where my piano students entered for lessons. I opened the patio door curtains, expecting to see a student. They'd been dropping off notes and cookies since Tuesday night.

No one was there.

Tap. Tap. Tap.

I looked down. The sparrow stood on the brick patio, tapping his beak against the glass door. I froze, holding my breath, not wanting to startle him. *Is this the same bird?* He hopped back a few steps and stared at me for a long moment, his head tilted. Then he seemed to nod. He turned and walked away.

"No!" I cried and wrenched open the door. The screech startled him, and he hopped faster, disappearing into the bushes. I crouched low, opening the branches, looking through the leaves, but I couldn't find him.

I'm not sure why I searched for so long. I didn't believe in signs or the story Michael was telling everyone. When I was young, my parents never spoke of signs. Heaven was this faraway place where our loved ones looked down on us. They were in our hearts, but not in our lives, not sending us little touches of magic. After my sister died, my parents rarely spoke of her. Sometimes, they'd tell us a memory. But they never glanced at the sky and said Elizabeth is the bird flying above. We never searched the ground, hoping she dropped a penny for us to find. I didn't even know people believed in that.

But that morning of my son's funeral, I needed something, anything, to get through the day. I didn't want to take the Valium my friends offered. But maybe, for a little bit, I could believe in this sparrow.

Just for that day, the day we buried our son, I allowed myself to believe. I didn't press my hands over my heart like Michael did with his bird; this was a story I kept hidden inside me, like a secret prescription stashed at the bottom of my pocketbook. Every few hours, I closed my eyes and remembered the bird knocking on my door, asking to be let in. And just for a moment, I believed, and a sense of peace washed over me.

19

I didn't pick out the hymns for Brendan's funeral. I didn't care because I didn't plan on singing. I didn't even plan on standing; I wasn't sure I'd have the strength. But when the pianist played a few chords, my muscles tightened, and I stood without thinking, the same way I did twenty years before, when I brought Michael to mass with me and my parents.

He was Jewish but not religious. He'd celebrated Christmas as a child with a cardboard fireplace and stockings filled with presents. His mother even dressed his sisters in Easter bonnets and dresses, charmed by the ribbons and ruffles of a Christian holiday. But, he'd never been inside a church before and was mystified by the dance around him.

"How do you know when to kneel? Or stand?" he whispered after we'd all knelt as one and then risen. He wanted a code word, some kind of signal, and after hearing the priest say the same words at least a thousand times, I should have known when to rise or kneel. The reflex was in my body, though, not my mind. My muscles moved without thought, my response buried deep within.

The same thing happened at Brendan's funeral. The pianist played a chord and suddenly I stood, filled with a sudden need to sing this song. I didn't even know the song, but I had to sing it. I scanned the bulletin for the hymn number.

"Quick, I need a hymnal," I whispered to Michael and he reached for one. I almost dropped it when he handed it to me. I flipped through the pages, my fingers fumbling. I grew breathless. I had to find it before the first word was sung. It needed to be perfect, but I couldn't find the page number. Finally, Michael handed me another book, opened to the correct page.

I stood tall, my shoulders back. I took a deep breath and sang. Tears blurred my eyes. My ribs tightened around me, squeezing until my words came out in little pants. My legs trembled, and I was about to give into the weakness. But behind me, I heard my father. Normally, he didn't stand, so he could conserve his energy for singing. But that day he stood. His deep voice rang out without even a hint of waver. He barely had enough oxygen to speak, but that day he used all of his strength for singing.

I didn't turn around, but I leaned into his bass notes. I could almost feel them rumbling inside me, grounding me. The ache in my ribs eased a bit. My voice grew steady.

There was no Amen at the end of the hymn. But it didn't matter. I sang, my voice strong and pure. My father's voice flowed around me, wrapping me in strength and together, we sang every last verse.

Modulation

Modulation is a key change in music. It adds interest and variety to a song. A pop song will often move into a key that's a step or two higher. Most people don't hear it. But they can feel it.

When the key changes, something moves inside me. I sense the lift moving me higher and higher. It's the same song, but something feels different. Brighter. It's as if a light is switched on.

It fills me with hope.

20

It was the night before the first day of school, seven days after Brendan had died. Zack and Lizzie sat on the floor of my room, going through their school backpacks. Lizzie held the list of supplies in her hand.

"I need Post-its," she said, and I walked down the two flights to the basement where I kept supplies on a shelf. Lizzie was entering fifth grade, Zack seventh. Earlier that day, I'd taken them to their school and spoken with their teachers and principals. The school was willing to give us time, whatever we needed, but Zack and Lizzie wanted to start school on time. They were eager for the distraction.

I stared at the notebooks, scissors, and tape. Normally, I loved new school supplies. I'd get chills down my back each time I opened a notebook, excited for a fresh start and new possibilities. But I couldn't think of the future, only the next thirty seconds. I grabbed the Post-its and used the few moments alone to cry silent tears that racked my ribs. When I climbed back up the stairs, my ribs ached, but my face was dry.

I did this for an hour, descending the two flights, to get one supply at a time, taking far too long. I remembered to smile each time I returned and watched them stuff their backpacks until the packs were fat with supplies. When we finished, the kids ran to their bathroom to wash up for bed.

I sat at the kitchen table, my head bowed, listening to the sounds of water running above me. I took deep breaths, not even looking up at the scrape of a kitchen chair. I thought it was Michael, back from walking Snowy.

After a moment, I looked up. It was Zack. He didn't say anything, didn't even meet my eyes. His fingers traced circles on the table. He wouldn't look at me so I stared down at my hands, hoping to make it easier for him. I counted his breaths while I waited. Finally, he spoke.

"Is Brendan in heaven?"

I closed my eyes for a second and then looked at him. "Of course he is. He's up in heaven with God."

We'd said it dozens of times. Before the funeral. After. At the cemetery when we watched the casket lower into the ground. We said it every night, when the dark made everything scarier and we dragged in their mattresses so they could sleep on the floor next to us. Even then, Zack and Lizzie fought to be the one closest to our bed.

"He's in heaven," I said again. "With my sister, Elizabeth. And Papa."

Zack shrugged and reached for a napkin. "I'm not sure anymore."

"Well, I am." I wasn't.

Oh, how I wanted to believe he was. When my sister died, I thought of heaven as this faraway place, beyond the clouds, beyond the stars. I thought of my sister as smiling down, watching me, surrounded by clouds and angels and anything she could ever want. As a mother, I wanted to believe my son was somewhere safe. I was desperate to believe that, but I was filled with doubts.

I said none of this to Zack. I touched his hand. "There's so much we're feeling right now. We're lost and heartbroken. But that's the one thing I know for sure. He's with God."

He tore the napkin in half and then in quarters. "But he never really talked about God. Or heaven. What if he didn't believe?"

His fingers moved faster, shredding the napkins into pieces. I waited, watching his shoulders tense and tighten until they touched his ears. "He didn't say the words, Mom. My friend said you need to say them if you want to get into heaven. You need to say you believe in God."

His voice broke and he looked at me, his eyes filled with tears. "Brendan didn't say the words."

I reached for a piece of his napkin. I almost took his hand, but I was afraid he'd push me off and run from the room. "Your friend is wrong. God doesn't need the words."

He looked down again, tearing his napkin into smaller pieces. Zack was so open with his emotions, whether it was anger or love. He'd run into the house, flushed from playing baseball and throw his arms around me, smelling of fresh air, his arms warmed from sunshine. "I love you," he'd say before running back outside.

And Lizzie couldn't stop talking about love. She'd spin herself around and throw herself onto the floor, her arms spread wide. "I can't take it anymore, Mama. My heart is too full with love."

But Brendan didn't have the words. He never ran to me and told me he loved me. He said it back if I said it first. He never hesitated saying it back, but it never burst out of him on his own. I didn't even notice it at first, not until Zack and Lizzie started saying it. I asked him once to say it first. He was eight and had come into the piano room and asked me what I wanted for my birthday.

"I want to give you something you want," he said. "And not just a card. How about a book? A gift card to a restaurant?"

I smiled at him. "I want you to say you love me. First. Before I say it."

"That's what you want?" He thought about it and then nodded. "Okay."

All day on my birthday, he crept around the house, looking at me sideways, struggling to say it. He didn't say it at dinner or after I read them stories at bedtime. Finally, I kissed him goodnight and walked back to my room. A few minutes later, he barreled in and flung himself into my arms.

"I love you," he whispered. He squeezed me hard. "There. I said it first. I love you."

He ran back to his bed. I never asked him to say it again. He showed me he loved me in so many ways. He always said it back, but it made him too self-conscious to say it first.

Zack shredded his napkin while I searched for the right thing to say. "Brendan had a hard time saying those words. But he *showed* love. That's more important. Like the silly wave he did for Lizzie. And remember last year, when you came home crying about your report card? He never said anything to you. But he dug out his old one from sixth grade to show you he didn't do great the first quarter either." Brendan had said nothing; just shoved the paper into Zack's face, showing him the evidence. "He couldn't stand seeing you in pain. That's love."

Zack stopped shredding the napkin and looked at me.

"Whenever I was upset, he'd make me coupons for a trip to the bookstore or a restaurant. Or sit next to me and hold my hand. He wasn't good at words." I laughed. "Sometimes, he was horrible at words. He knew that. But he was good, oh, so good at showing his love."

I dropped my piece of napkin and reached for Zack's hand, squeezing gently. "Remember last Monday?" I asked and then stopped for a second. *Our last full day with Brendan.*

"I wasn't feeling well and he made me tuna and crackers for lunch.

Without me even asking." He'd added a splash of vinegar because that's how I taught him. Only he didn't trust a splash and insisted on measuring it out with a teaspoon. "He even made me a limeade." He'd spent all summer perfecting his recipe.

Suddenly, I stood up and walked into the den. I'd forgotten that I put the bowl on the bookshelf. It was still there, hidden behind the chair. *That was only eight days ago.* It seemed like a lifetime ago. I picked up the bowl, holding it to my chest as I walked back to Zack.

The bowl spun a little as I put it on the table. I waited until the rocking stopped. "That's love." I pointed to the dried up tuna. "He might not have talked about love, but that's okay because he felt it. And he showed it. That's what matters to God. Not the words."

Zack drew in a breath and let out the air in a long whistle. He giggled at the sound and I smiled with him. He flicked the metal bowl and made it spin and rock. His breathing slowed.

I can do this. I can make my children feel better. I wasn't sure what I believed. My own grief was a huge expanse of darkness in front of me, but easing their fears was something I knew how to do. It made me feel strong.

"I need colored pencils," Lizzie called from upstairs.

Zack jumped up. "I think I need them, too. Let me check." He ran up the stairs.

"Got it," I yelled. I reached across the table and gathered up the tiny bits of napkin, crushing them together in my hand. I placed the tuna fish bowl into the sink. Then I went downstairs and grabbed the boxes of colored pencils. I wiped away my tears, took a deep breath and climbed the stairs to my children, one step at a time.

On their first day of school, I stayed in bed until I heard the whine of the school bus pulling into our development. It was the high school bus, the one Brendan should have been on. I waited until the squeal of brakes faded away and then got up.

I poured cereal and packed peanut butter sandwiches, slipping little notes inside their lunch bags. I drew a funny face on Zack's note and filled Lizzie's with hearts and flowers before grabbing the camera and taking pictures. Zack left first. He wouldn't let me walk him down the block, wouldn't even let me come out onto the front steps, but Lizzie held my hand as she skipped down the hill.

"Mommy, Miss McCormick is so pretty," she said. "She has long hair and pretty eyes. I'm going to have the best year ever."

I shivered at the icy trickle inside me, but I smiled and squeezed her hand. *The best year ever? How could she say that?*

But I remembered at my sister's wake, my cousins and I had snuck down into the basement, playing hide-and-go-seek in the maze of rooms. We shrieked with laughter. As children, we felt the sadness, but it was easy to shrug off. We didn't carry the sorrow into moments of joy.

Lizzie and I waited for the bus to stop and open its door. She climbed on, never looking back until she settled into her seat. I waved her off and then walked up the hill. Michael was on the front lawn, Snowy on the leash.

"Let's go to the trail," I said.

We'd taken the kids to the Columbia Trail a few times, walking on a gravel path through a canopy of trees. I needed to be surrounded by trees, to feel some small measure of peace. The sky was filled with gray clouds and there was a heaviness in the air, but I didn't care. We drove to the trail and walked for miles. Rain drizzled down on us, but we kept walking, not talking, the only sound was the rustling of leaves. When we reached a group of gray boulders, Michael stopped. He leaned over the rocks, his hands on the rough surface, gasping for air.

"I have to know if he's okay. If he's in heaven. Please." He reached out blindly, searching for my hand. "Tell me he's okay."

I'd convinced Zack the night before, but Michael wouldn't be as easy. He'd asked me this a few times each day, begging me to explain the rules of religion to him. He'd grown up without religion, without any dogma. After all my years of catechism, I no longer believed in rules. Like Brendan, I had no patience for dogma.

"I follow the rules of science," Brendan said once. "That's my religion."

I thought I believed he was in heaven last night, but each time Michael asked me this question, a kernel of doubt slipped in. Brendan was never confirmed as a Catholic. What if there were some kind of test, something he could fail? *Was loving God enough?*

I ached for someone to comfort me, to make me believe Brendan was in heaven. I didn't say what I was thinking. Instead, I patted Michael's shoulder, soothing him with the same words I'd used with Zack. His shaking eased, and his breathing slowed while the rain grew heavy. I rubbed circles on his back and stared at the drops of rain on my hand. Michael took a deep breath in and stood up from the rock. He looked up at the darkened sky. "Do you want to head back?"

"No. Let's keep going."

We had walked for a half mile when I saw a flash of silver ahead. I squinted through the rain. A woman on a bike rode toward us. The bike was old-fashioned with a basket and big round wheels, as if she were out delivering pies to everyone in the village.

Waving, she took her feet off the pedals, coasted over the gravel, and grinned. "Let it rain," she said, looking up at the sky. We nodded. She passed us, and I turned to watch her ride away, thinking how strange she was. She almost seemed to flicker in the rain.

She laughed and held up her hand, catching raindrops. "The gates of heaven are opening up," she shouted over her shoulder. "The gates of heaven!"

Her voice echoed as we watched her disappear down the trail.

The gates of heaven. I shook the water from my ear.

"What did she say?" I asked.

Michael grinned, the same smile he had when he cupped the bird in his hands. "The gates of heaven are opening up!" He started laughing. "The gates of heaven are opening up. Oh, it's a sign."

We turned around and headed back toward our car. The rain poured down. We were soaked. My legs felt heavy, but an urgency pushed us forward. I don't know why, but we walked fast, then faster, until we were running through the rain. I grew breathless, but Michael was a runner and he kept talking.

"The gates of heaven," he said every few steps. "They're opening up." He paused and listened for a moment. There was only the squish of our sneakers and the leaves rustling with rain, but he clapped his hands as if the trees answered us back.

I could still hear her words. I was cold and wet and heavy with darkness, but something inside me lifted. We ran to our car and slid in. I couldn't catch my breath. My ribs ached and I wrapped my arms around my belly, trying to slow my panting.

After a few minutes, the rain stopped and our breaths slowed. We sat in silence and still I heard her words. *The gates of heaven are opening up.*

Suddenly, Michael gasped and pointed. "Look, there's a bird."

On the ground in front of us was a bird. He was brown and looked like a wren. There was nothing special about this bird. He looked at us and tilted his head like all birds do. And yet, he seemed to shimmer just like the woman shouting about heaven.

We stared at him for a long time. Finally, Michael turned on the car and still the bird sat there. We started humming to the song playing on the radio and then looked at each other when we realized the words. It was all about getting ready to believe.

I nodded at the bird, smiling when he nodded back.

Maybe I can believe.

I started to laugh. I grabbed Michael's hand and we held onto each other, listening to the song and staring at the bird. We laughed, howls that shook the car. It started raining again and still, we couldn't stop laughing. The bird stared at us. We shivered from the cold rain and laughed until we cried.

21

Michael became convinced that Brendan kept sending us songs. I shivered in the car that day, singing the words about getting ready to believe. But it was easy for me to dismiss it as coincidence, easy for logic to take over. "How could he control the airwaves?" I asked Michael. It made no sense to me. Besides, Brendan didn't even like music.

When Brendan was five, I took his hand, and we walked down the basement stairs to my piano studio. He'd been in it many times before, but this would be his first official lesson. The day before, he'd helped me unroll the new music rug in the middle of the floor.

He hopped from square to square on the rug, each one stamped with a musical symbol. He named them all, from the treble clef to the accent note. He even remembered the fermata symbol, the one for holding a note longer. "I'm staying here a bit longer. Get it?" he asked before laughing and jumping to the half note.

But when the three other students walked in, Brendan refused to tap rhythms on the drum. He never swished his scarf to the music or bounced the ball to the beat. He sat on his square shaking his head no.

I'd built a reputation as a teacher; I was the piano whisperer, the one who could get any child to love music. I was patient with the little girl who chewed on her hair and insisted on calling me Miss Lisa instead of Linda. I even wrote a song for her about mixing up names. I had no problems with the boy whose entire goal was to escape the room. I knew exactly how to engage each child.

Except for Brendan. As a teacher, I knew he needed to observe, that it might take months before he'd participate. But as a parent it was nearly impossible, especially when the three other students did everything.

"Just let him sit and watch," Michael said. It's what I told myself each class, but I couldn't seem to find the patience that was so unlimited for my other students. When the parents came back to participate in the last ten minutes, my cheeks flushed hot because Brendan wouldn't echo rhythms or sing the goodbye song. He sat on his square, rocking back and forth, lost in his own world.

One afternoon, he was sick and stayed upstairs during class. The next week, he looked tired so I suggested he stay upstairs again. He ran to the couch and stretched out, smiling as he stared at his animals. The following week, I said nothing and went down the stairs by myself. He never asked about it.

"We'll try again in a few months," I told Michael, but it took me nearly two more years before I tried again, and really, only because Zack was starting piano. This time, it worked. Something clicked in Brendan, the logic, the rules of music.

"I got it," he'd say, nodding his head and waving me away. He could read both hands together, find the patterns, play the chords. I moved him into private lessons, this time because he outpaced the class.

But he never felt the emotions of the song, never heard its stories. I used to take colored pencils and shade the song for him. Light pink for quiet, red for power, blue for playful. He almost convinced me he felt the song. He'd lean in, and float his hands off the keys, but only because I'd written that in. He didn't feel the song, not even as he got older. I tried to make him love music. I bought him an iPod, but he only put two songs on it. We took him to a video game concert, hoping the music would lure him in, but he only stared at the screens, watching the graphics flash on and off.

Music was math to him, a formula to figure out. He learned Billy Joel's "Root Beer Rag," but after the recital, he never played it again.

"Why should I? It's done," he said, as if the music were a crossword already puzzled out.

He didn't like music. That was the excuse I used to not believe. It didn't matter to Michael. "Who cares? Brendan loves music now," he said. Each day, Michael visited the cemetery and came home with song titles scribbled on the back of receipts and deposit slips. He walked into the house like some mad scientist, his arm held high in victory, his hand still clutching the scrap of paper. "I got a new one today. 'Open the Door to Your Heart.'" He waved the paper in front of me.

"See, right here. It says just listen to the words and open the door to your heart." He looked up at me, his eyes begging me to believe. "We need to keep our hearts open."

He put the song into a playlist, a special one just for the songs he believed Brendan sent him. Soon, it grew so large he split it into three lists. Michael lived in this world of magic, one where Brendan listened to him and sent him messages. It always began with a question. *Are you around me?* He'd wait for a response. An hour later, he burst into the house with his slip of paper. "I turned on the car and "Hello, It's Me" came on. Don't you see? He's answering me. He's saying, Hello, I'm always around."

He shook his head when I said nothing.

It didn't stop him from walking into the house with new songs. I didn't believe, and yet I pored over the lyrics with him and played them continuously on my iPad.

But numbers, not songs, were where I found my comfort. I searched inside numbers, hoping their power would move me toward something. I started with a row of numbers, counting the weeks since I'd lost him. Then I'd count the days, the hours, sometimes even the minutes and then the seconds, knowing I'd have to start all over again. I stared at the long row of numbers as if they held the secret. I didn't know what I believed in anymore, but, oh, I still had faith in numbers.

Michael had read it took three years for parents to regain their balance after the loss of their child; I was determined to beat that number. I spent hours crafting the perfect spreadsheet, searching for a formula to navigate through grief. *What if I walked a 10K? And I did it ten times? What if I learned a new song on the piano? How many would I need to learn? What about lunch with friends? Would that help?*

I played with the possibilities. I sat at my kitchen table and made a chart. Sometimes I was convinced I'd found it. I walked a few 10Ks with Michael's sister Hedy and painted a craft project and then colored in the boxes on my chart. But always, after a week or so, I ripped up my plan and reached for another piece of paper. *Maybe if I started my day with a walk in the woods and ended with reading a book?* I drew a new grid and stared at the empty rows. For hours each day, I played with the possibilities of numbers, searching for that elusive formula that was always out of my reach.

It was Mrs. Bain, my first piano teacher, who taught me that music was based on math and numbers. I held my breath the first time she showed me sheet music filled with dots and squiggly lines, a secret code I learned to decipher years before algebra. During our lessons, I sat on the piano bench, Mrs. Bain sitting on my right in our dining room chair. When she listened to me play, she'd tilt her head and close her eyes. Sometimes, I thought she was sleeping, but after I'd finished, she'd memorized every note I'd played. *Softer here,* she'd say, circling a few notes with her pencil. *More legato here.* Then, she'd wait for my questions. She always knew the answer.

"Why does this song make me sad?" I asked. And she smiled and explained about minor keys and the formula of intervals that made a chord. She played a major chord and then a minor one, changing only one note, but that one small half step down added a wash of blue that made tears well in my eyes.

"Why does this song make me want to spin around the room?" And I learned about triplets and the pulse of music, a drumbeat inside that echoes the rhythm and pushes you to move. Fast triplets made me want to whirl around the room, but slow ones made me sway and glide in a waltz. It all came down to numbers and it seemed like magic to me.

One day, she moved off her chair and slid onto the bench next to me and taught me about cadences, a progression of chords that move to an ending. In each key, a chord is numbered from one to seven.

"Feel how the five chord moves you to the one." She played a few chords and then lingered on the last one, laughing when I started to wiggle. "That's the dominant, or the five chord. You can't end a song on this. It's unfinished. Listen."

She played the chords for Happy Birthday while singing. She slowed down on the last line.

Happy Birthday to—

She stayed on the word "to," drawing it out until her voice faded away but I could still hear the chord. I closed my eyes and felt the magnetic pull inside me. There was only silence, but I swayed on the bench and kicked my legs when the suspense became too much. I opened my eyes, reached out, and played the C chord while I sang the word *you*. I had to finish the song.

She smiled. "See? Songs need to end on the one chord. That's our home key. A cadence is powerful because the five chord leads you back to the one, the home key. We call this a perfect cadence."

All week, I practiced moving from the five chord to the one, in twelve different keys. And it was perfect. I loved feeling the pull that dragged me from one chord to another. The following week, Mrs. Bain slid back onto my bench and showed me a different cadence.

"Now listen to this one. This is the four-chord moving to the one. It's the plagal cadence. It still moves you to the home key, but a bit gentler."

I closed my eyes. There was still a pull, but it felt more like a slide. She played it again and my eyes flew open. I knew this cadence.

"It's the Amen," I whispered.

We sang it at church, at the end of each hymn. Each time that Amen filled the space within me, filled me with a sense of mystery. Now I knew why. This was the magic. This was music and numbers adding up to so much more than its parts.

Amen means *I believe.* It ends the prayer with an exclamation point, underscoring that these words are true. *I believe.* And I believed. I'm not sure why. I was the little scientist in my house, the one who asked so many questions growing up. I set up my own laboratory in my bedroom, with a microscope and notebook stuffed with experiments. I never stopped asking why.

Except when it came to faith. Like the rituals knitted into my muscles, faith had seeped into my mind, taking over until I accepted everything I was told from the church five houses down. For months, I played the plagal cadence on my piano. Sometimes, I didn't even sit on the bench. I stood before my piano and reached for the keys, smiling at the power building inside me. It made me stand on my tippy toes, as I reached higher and higher, hearing that Amen with every part of my soul, waiting to be led home.

But now? I stared at the numbers on my grief spreadsheet. I no longer believed in the Amen and its magic. Only numbers.

22

After Michael and I were engaged, my parents gave us a menorah for Christmas. They had spoken their concerns over me marrying outside of my faith; this was their way of offering acceptance. I thought I'd get married at the wedding hall, but my mother's eyes teared each time she talked of me walking down the aisle at Saint Raphael's Church. So Michael and I walked down the block and filled out the form for a dispensation for me to marry a Jew. The only requirement? I had to sign something promising to raise our children Catholic.

I tried. I really did.

All three of my children were baptized at St. Elizabeth's, a church only a few blocks away from our house. When Brendan was six, I enrolled him in catechism class even though we rarely attended Sunday mass. Each week, I examined the parent handbook, trying to figure out a way to answer his questions without revealing my own doubts. When he turned eight, it was Michael who took him to his communion workshop. It was a scavenger hunt, the kind where you searched for religious symbols inside the church. Michael had no problem hunting for something he didn't understand.

After Brendan made his communion, we drank juice and wandered the hall. The children had written letters to Jesus. They were taped to the wall. Most thanked him for his love, with red hearts drawn around their words. Brendan's letter was a question, wondering how he could have survived forty days in a desert without food and water.

"Maybe food," he told me later. "But there's no way he went that long without water. Forty days? Where's the science?" He shrugged his shoulders and walked away. A few years later, I let him quit his catechism class.

But he did go to a Bible camp the summer he turned twelve, mostly because friends of Zack had signed up, and I was looking for something to get them out of the house. It was two weeks filled with crafts and sports and a giant tarp for slipping down their hill. Lizzie went too, and all three kids came home tired, with skinned knees and muddy elbows. They shrugged when I asked them what they'd learned.

I found out the following year when we went to West Virginia.

I couldn't handle another vacation standing in line at Disney, so I'd booked an adventure trip, filled with mountain climbing and cliff jumping. Lizzie was only eight but eager to keep up with her brothers. Michael and the boys rappelled down an eighty-foot mountain while Lizzie and I hiked through the woods and got massages in a yurt. We kayaked in a lake, sailed through trees on a zip line, and spent a terrifying hour clutching paddles while we rafted in the rapids. We explored a new adventure every day, and yet for me, the most memorable part of the trip was the afternoon we stopped for pizza.

The smell of wood smoking and yeasty bread distracted me as the five of us walked through the maze of tables into the back room. I ignored the murmur of the boys' voices as we sat down and I studied the menu. Michael ordered appetizers, probably hoping food would distract the boys. It sounded like another argument, but I was too busy trying to decide between a pizza piled with artichoke hearts and olives or shrimp scampi.

When I looked up, Brendan's face was red. This wasn't a spat over who sits where.

Brendan shook his head. "Science is wrong?" His voice crescendoed with each word. "Science is wrong? I can't believe this."

He slapped his hands on the table. I stared at him, shocked. He hated drawing attention to himself in public. He never let a restaurant know it was his birthday for fear of a line of waiters clapping and singing. He even cringed if the table next to him had a birthday. But right now, he didn't care that the waitress was standing there with a platter full of wings and garlic knots. He didn't even notice when she put them on the table and quickly left. He stood up, his chair falling backward. I steadied his chair. He leaned over the table. "Science. Is. Not. Wrong."

Zack said nothing, a smug smile on his face. Lizzie's eyes were wide as her head swung back from brother to brother. Zack reached for a wing and shrugged, a gesture designed to torment.

"You don't believe in science? That . . . that—" Brendan trembled, his chest heaving up and down. I put my hand on his arm, but he shrugged it off. "Science." He drew the word out in a long hiss. "You have to believe in science."

Zack shook his head. "Nope. I don't even believe in evolution. I believe in God." He dipped his wing into a puddle of blue cheese dressing, dismissing his brother.

"Evolution is fake," Lizzie said. "That's what they told us at the church camp."

"Exactly," Zack said.

Brendan's face purpled. He opened his mouth, but no words came out. Michael picked up the platter and put a few garlic knots on Brendan's plate. Brendan shook his head, but then the smell of garlic butter and parmesan cheese broke through his outrage. He sank slowly into the chair and reached for a garlic knot.

He took a bite and then another. He leaned back in his chair, calm now. He smirked. "I have news for you, Zack. The gorge we hiked this morning? It was carved from water millions of years ago."

Zack shook his head. "Nope."

For a second, it looked like Brendan would argue. But then he shrugged and reached for the wings, their argument forgotten.

But I couldn't forget it. We rarely went to church, rarely discussed faith. I was so filled with resentment that I'd left a spiritual vacuum. Each boy had swung as far to the other side as they could. Zack believed the earth was only six thousand years old. Brendan was on his way to becoming an atheist who worshipped only science. Lizzie switched her beliefs, based on whichever brother was whispering in her ear.

I needed to do something. By the time dessert came, I'd made a plan. I came home from the vacation determined to find a way to fill our spiritual vacuum. I'd find us a church, one that wasn't filled with rules or dogma. But by the time we came home, my plan was forgotten, easily swept away by the demands of teaching full-time and juggling three kids.

That fall, Michael and I waited until all three kids were at school, and then we drove into the city. While he worked in his office, I walked down Fifth Avenue, weaving my way through the crowds. None of the stores called to me, not even to window-shop. I stopped when I saw St. Thomas Church. I walked up the stone steps, pulled by the open door. There were a few people scattered in the pews. I walked up the aisle and slid into an empty one. I was surrounded by stained glass and statues carved from stone and arches that pointed toward the heavens. Candlelight flickered on the walls.

I brushed my hand against the warm wood, surprised at the stirring within me. It was more than just the beauty that filled me. I was alone and yet felt a presence.

I sat there for a long time. For the first time since I was a teenager, a yearning flowed through me, a current stronger than anger. I felt it build inside me. I welcomed it. There were hymnals scattered in the pews, but I didn't pick them up. I sat with my hands in my lap, my eyes closed, silence all around me. I couldn't think of anything to say. I heard nothing in return, not even a whisper. Still, something touched my soul.

It felt like a prayer.

I came home with the knowledge that something was missing in my life. But I still wasn't ready to go to church. I researched religion. I collected dozens of books and spent a year flipping through them, trying to find something I could believe in. In the end, I had no answers. Nothing I could point to and say, *Yes. This. This is what I believe.*

But that ache grew until it woke me up at night, an edgy anxiety that made me make a list of all the churches in our area. Finally, a few weeks after Brendan turned fourteen, we visited a church inside a school. Somehow that made it seem easier, as if I were going to a PTA meeting instead of trying to find God. Once we visited that church, I felt giddy with freedom. In the Catholic church, you attended your parish, like a school district. But now, we could visit any church we wanted.

Every month we tested out a new church. Afterward, we ate

breakfast in a diner and talked about the church. The kids voted for their favorite. We had the Starbucks Church because they served coffee and donuts before service. The Too Friendly Church Brendan named because a line of people shook our hands and even chased us in the parking lot to shake them again. Lizzie loved the Carnival Church, which had a children's program that included balloons and a DJ and, once, a giant machine that spun cotton candy. And then my favorite, The Music Church, complete with guitars, drummers, singers, even a horn section. Zack loved the saxophone player. We never stayed long at these churches. There was always another church to try, another book to read, another religion to research.

23

I had trouble sleeping during the summer when Brendan turned fifteen. I kept waking up in a sweat. I'd been searching for a church for almost a year. It was no longer a yearning inside me, but a sense of urgency that made me breathless. I needed to find a church and yet I rejected almost every one I found.

But in August, I made an announcement at dinner. "It turns out, we're Presbyterians. We'll go to the one in town this Sunday." It wasn't their rules or dogma that attracted me, but that their power wasn't in bishops and cardinals thousands of miles away. They believed in governing by small groups in their congregation.

The kids looked at me, waiting. I sighed. "Yes, we'll go to the diner after." They didn't really care where I took them, as long as food was involved.

It was only Michael, Zack, and I the first Sunday we went to the United Presbyterian Church in town. Lizzie was sick and stayed with Brendan, snuggling inside his bed. We pulled into the parking lot, surprised when we saw people walking toward a large wooden pavilion surrounded by trees. It looked like a nice place for an afternoon picnic.

I'd gotten used to different church environments, but as a lapsed Catholic, church still meant dabbing on holy water before slipping into pews that smelled like lemon oil. Church was light streaming in through the stained-glass windows and smoky incense that tickled my nose. There was ceremony and a sense of formality that I wasn't sure I could find in a hot backyard with the scent of freshly mowed grass and people flapping their church bulletins at the flies around them.

I tugged on Michael's arm. "Let's go," I whispered. We climbed back into our car before anyone noticed us. But we came back the following Sunday. I couldn't silence that voice inside my head. It was only Michael and I who came. I felt nervous and didn't want the kids to notice that. The service was indoors this time. The church was simple but larger than I thought, with handmade banners hanging on the walls. Their main decoration was a large wooden cross hanging from the ceiling.

Organ music filled the room with hymns, different from my childhood, but familiar enough. The people were nice, like in all the churches we visited, turning around to shake our hands and chat about the weather. But it was the sermon that caught my attention. Not because of the subject. Halfway through the sermon, the minister stopped and frowned. "I've forgotten my watch. Can someone let me know when ten minutes is up?"

The sermons we'd heard this past year were long. Zack and Lizzie usually went into the children's program, but not Brendan. He sat next to me, fidgeting and rocking until his plastic chair squeaked. He took balls of lint off his sock and put them on my leg. "Are they done yet?" he whispered.

But this minister had a time limit. "Got it," someone called from the side of the church. He went back to his sermon. After a few minutes, she called out, "Five more minutes." When his time was up, she yelled out, "That's it!"

Michael and I looked at each other, smiling. Brendan would have no problem standing up, stopwatch in hand, calling out his warnings. He wouldn't let him speak even a second over his allotted time. After the service, we spent some time talking with people and meeting the minister, Rev. Rick. When we got into our car, Michael smiled at me. There was nothing that different from all the other churches. But something seemed so right, a feeling neither one of us could explain. I reached for Michael's hand. "I think we finally found our church."

It wasn't that I suddenly believed in all the rules of religion. I wasn't filled with the presence of God. The organist didn't even play the Amen after the hymns, but still, I felt as if I were coming home.

We stopped at the store and bought a box of jelly donuts for the kids. It felt like a celebration. It wasn't just the church. I was finally moving a step closer to God.

A year earlier, my yearning had been greater than the anger I'd nursed since I was fourteen. But now, my anger melted away. Not even a little of it. All of it. A giddiness swooshed into its place. I burst into our house, box of donuts in hand. I was ready to belong to something bigger than me.

"We're home," I called out. "We have donuts. And a new church." The kids ran down the stairs and I hugged each one and told them all about our new church.

"I want to go," Lizzie said, powder sugar sprinkled all over her nose. The boys just reached for another donut.

"We're all going to go next week," I said. "The five of us." I was so happy.

Six days later, the four of us returned for Brendan's funeral.

24

I found the first one in September. It was at the bottom of my tote bag, the one I used for teaching piano. I was getting ready to ease back into teaching, with only a small group of students. I reached inside, fumbling for a pencil, when I felt it. It was hard and small, barely an inch long. I rolled it between my fingers and traced its outline. I knew what it was, but I wasn't sure I could trust what I felt.

My fingers curled around it and finally, I moved my hand out of my bag. I held it in the palm of my hand. A wooden bird. It was painted a dusky blue with an orangey pink beak and a smile that made it seem so cheerful.

Each September, I hung a plaque from our coat closet door knob. HAPPY FALL, it read, its blue wooden birds dangling off the bottom. I often leaned my bag against the door; it wasn't hard to imagine a loose bird dropping into my bag.

I didn't tell Michael. I didn't want to hear his gasp or see the wonder in his eyes. Still, I stared at this bird for a long time. I didn't hang up the plaque this fall, so I must have been carrying the bird around in my bag for a year. I'd reached into this bag almost every day that I taught piano, but I never once noticed it. After staring at it for so long, I gently placed it back into my bag.

I reached for it, sometimes. Like the day I taught a little boy how to play a Halloween song. I'd forgotten that I taught Brendan the same song, and the memories rushed over me. I saw Brendan's hand reach high on the piano, his two fingers pressing against the black keys for the witch's cackle. He moved lower and played the spooky growl that always made him turn to me and laugh.

This little boy's giggle broke the spell. He sounded nothing like Brendan. I squeezed the bird until the beak bit into my palm, until that small pain pushed aside the memories. I smiled at the little boy and peeled off a jack-o'-lantern sticker and placed it on his music.

25

In mid-September, my parents came to visit. My dad stood tall, his shoulders pushed back with stoic determination. He didn't carry his toolbox, but he wore his Daddy fix face. It was the same face he had the night after the bird had come for the first time. He had his own bird story. "The bird came up to me when I took out the garbage," he'd said, his voice filled with forced cheer. "He said hello to me."

My father didn't believe in signs, but he had been desperate to do anything to fix my pain.

He still was. He smiled. "Just say the word and we'll start knocking down kitchen cabinets," he said as they stood in the hallway. He carried a fistful of brochures with glossy pictures of kitchen counters, convinced a remodeling project would distract me.

Maybe it would. I couldn't sit with my sorrow. Michael's family could. They sat with us at the table for hours, his mother's hand on mine, sometimes not even talking. They were so comfortable in letting their grief swallow them. Even in public. His sister Eileen had once thrown herself on her grandmother's grave. I couldn't do that. And yet, I knew if I fell to my knees, Eileen would kneel next to me, and together we'd rock back and forth, moved by the rhythm of grief.

Sometimes I wanted to. Loss weighed me down, settled inside my chest until I could barely take a breath. But it also filled me with an edgy anxiety. I needed to move. That's how my family dealt with grief.

We needed action. My mother had taken away Elizabeth's bed within a few days. My father turned his office—the room next to mine—into a bedroom for Jimmy. He opened up the back of Elizabeth's closet so Jimmy could have one in his room. He hung sheetrock over the opening on my side of the room, plastering and painting until Elizabeth's closet disappeared, like it had never been there.

That's what I needed to do now. Move. I'd spent hours scraping the ceiling in Lizzie's bedroom, trying to fix an old leak. But I needed more. My father handed me a brochure. For a moment, I considered it. I wanted to take a sledgehammer to the kitchen cabinets, punch holes in the wall and break the countertop into tiny pieces. But destruction was the easy part; I didn't have the strength to rebuild, to imagine the future and see what the kitchen could look like. I couldn't plan more than an hour ahead. We'd be surrounded by rubble, living with the broken pieces all around us.

I waved my parents into the kitchen, about to offer coffee, but then I noticed my mother and the bright slash of red lipstick she wore. Rage slipped inside me, and for a moment, I welcomed it as it nudged away a bit of my grief.

How could she?

Her lipstick was perfect. It screamed, *Look at me. I have a steady hand. I'm doing okay.* I studied her as I grabbed the coffee mugs. Everything about her echoed the same message. Hairspray controlling the waves in her hair. Her face, calm. Scrubbed clean of any tears, as if she'd had her cry early in the morning, and that would be all she would allow herself for the day. Her back was straight; nothing weighed her down. She held herself strong, steel woven through her spine.

I couldn't even wear flashes of color, except for the bits of dried plaster scattered on the black leggings I'd worn all week long. I could barely brush the tangles from my hair. At night, I resented brushing my teeth, as if I had no right to that minty, fresh feeling.

And yet, my mother was able to face herself in the mirror and brush on a perfect layer of color.

My earliest memory is of my mother sitting at her vanity table, putting on lipstick. Elizabeth and I used to stand behind our mother's white stool, watching in the mirror as she filled in her lips with color. Her vanity table was small, with a white ruffled skirt and a mirrored top. "It's kidney shaped," she told me once, and I thought that was so sophisticated, furniture named after body parts. I'd seen pictures of her with long dresses, her hair teased high, wearing silver gloves that shimmered all the way to her elbow.

I was thirteen when I snuck into her room and sat at her vanity. She had brushes and sharpened pencils for eyebrows and little pots of eyeshadow that sparkled. I reached for one of the fluffy brushes, pretending to powder away the freckles dusting my cheeks. I slowly pressed down on the perfume bottle until a tiny drop landed on my finger and then dabbed behind my ears, just like my mother did. And just as my mother did every morning, I leaned forward and read the poem tucked into the frame of her mirror.

Lord, grant me the serenity to accept the things I cannot change;
The courage to change the things I can;
And the wisdom to know the difference.

I knew serenity meant peace, something I thought I understood at the time. Peace meant not fighting with my brothers or letting my sister eat the last cookie or accepting that I'd never get my hair to flip like the girls who sat with boys at the cool table.

Peace seemed like the penance the priest would hand out after you confessed your sins. *Say three Hail Marys and help your mother with dinner. Two Our Fathers and help your brother clean up his room.* Peace was something you had to work on, but it seemed easy enough to do.

But, this was before I understood how sick my sister was. I didn't know why my mother sat in front of the mirror each morning, asking God for serenity, courage, and wisdom. This was before I knew peace was the hardest one of all.

She forgot to put on her lipstick once. My sister and I were in the car, I in the front seat, Elizabeth stretched out in the back. I was fourteen, Elizabeth twelve. We were on our way to the hospital for a doctor's visit for her.

My mother came out of the house and climbed into the front seat. She handed me her pocketbook and then shifted the car into reverse, pushing herself up so she could swing her arm around the back of my seat. She caught sight of her reflection in the rearview mirror.

She slammed her foot on the brake. "Oh, my goodness. I forgot to put on lipstick."

She threw the car into park and rummaged through her pocketbook. "I can't find it." Finally, she drew out a tube and opened it up. She leaned into the mirror and then shook her head. "I can't wear this. It's the wrong color."

She tossed her pocketbook onto my lap. She ran into the house. She came back a minute later, smiling because she wore the perfect shade of lipstick.

We drove to the hospital. Elizabeth hated going there but I loved watching the doctors and the way my nose twitched from the sting of alcohol. I wanted to be a doctor. I saw medicine as a giant puzzle to solve. When they drew blood from her arm that day, I leaned forward, and watched her blood snake through the tube, drawing out her inner secrets.

My mother cried on the way home that day, gentle tears that leaked from the corner of her eyes and disappeared into her neck before she could wipe them away. Her hands clutched the steering wheel and her ribs quivered as she held in silent sobs. After a few minutes, I finally asked, "What's wrong?"

She glanced at my sister sleeping in the backseat. She shook her head. "Nothing." There was no tremor in her voice, and I smiled, thinking everything was all right. She said something else, something I didn't hear. She might have said, "There's dust in my eyes." Or maybe she told me that the song on the radio reminded her of my grandmother.

It didn't really matter what she said because she smiled at me, her lipstick perfect. I was young enough to believe her.

My parents and I spent the morning cleaning Brendan's room, doing laundry, and trying to keep busy. We never sat down. When it was time to go, my father reached for his brochures. He held them up. "Anytime you're ready," he said. "Just say the word and I'll be here."

My mother slipped on her jacket, brushing the collar into place. Suddenly, she jerked and reached for the banister on the stairs. Her fingers turned white as she held on, gathering strength. *Be strong,* she'd whispered to me the day Brendan died. I knew she was saying those same words to herself, willing herself to be strong for me.

After a minute, she took her hand away from the banister and nodded. "I promised him I wouldn't cry today," she said, tilting her head toward my father.

Tears welled in her eyes, but she wouldn't let them spill over. She'd had a lifetime of pushing them away. She took a quick breath and kissed me and then straightened her shoulders as she walked away, her cheeks dry, her lipstick perfect.

26

We had no real history with the United Presbyterian Church, nothing beyond staring at the wooden cross that hung above Brendan's casket. We were strangers there, and still they sent us meals and sympathy cards and knitted prayer shawls. The church made me remember what I'd lost, an ache that was nearly unbearable, and yet, we came back each week. A part of me liked being surrounded by strangers. Friends felt free to offer an avalanche of advice, but strangers simply nodded or reached for my hand.

I was there for the music, the hymns the organist played. Most were unfamiliar to me, but it didn't matter. I was pulled by something inside me that moved to the music, a small moment of peace. I gripped the wooden pew in front of me and rose each time those opening chords sounded, singing with the congregation, my voice strong and pure. I couldn't sing by myself, but here, I could sing with strangers.

The first week, there was a soloist, an older man with white hair, who stood as if he'd had years of military training. He sang like my father did. He took a deep breath, and his words burst out of him, a loud boom that gradually softened until he reached the end of the phrase. His voice filled the church. I glanced down at the bulletin. His name was Bob.

I need to sing with him.

A yearning washed over me. Surprised, I looked over at Michael and the kids, but they didn't notice anything. I hadn't sung with a choir since high school. I'd sung the hymns at Brendan's funeral, but since then, I couldn't even sing in front of Zack and Lizzie. I sang by myself when no one was home.

And yet, suddenly I saw myself, standing next to Bob, facing a church full of strangers, singing with him. I could almost hear our song, a soprano and tenor mixed together. It filled me with light. But then fear rushed in.

My throat tightened and my legs began to shake. Michael put his hand on my knee and I smiled at him, pretending everything was fine.

I'd closed my piano, convinced I'd never play again. But that didn't last. I kept hearing music inside me, a phrase that swirled around my head until I grew dizzy. In the past, I'd gone weeks before without playing. I had vacations and injuries and days where I barely touched the piano. But now it felt like an ache inside me, one that pulled me from sleep. My mind resisted even the idea of one note, but my body wouldn't listen. My legs shook until finally I walked to the piano. Slowly at first, one step at a time, and then faster until I stood before it.

I reached out to open it, but froze in midair. I wanted to touch the keys, wanted to feel their comfort, but I only stood there, the same way I stood behind the window watching Michael scoop up his bird of light. There was something here. I could almost feel the vibrations of the piano playing itself. I wanted to move forward, to let the sound waves wash over me like a lullaby rocking me to sleep.

I didn't move. My body begged and trembled, but my mind refused to give in to the ache. The last time I'd felt this way, I was six and starting piano lessons with Mrs. Bain the next morning. It was the middle of the night, and I'd crept down the stairs, sleepwalking. My mother told me the next day that I'd stood in front of the piano. She stopped me before I could play a note. I don't remember anything of that night, except the yearning inside me as I reached for the keys.

That's what I felt now as I stood over my closed piano, listening to a melody that had stirred me from sleep. I was alone in the house. But I was afraid to give in to the ache. I'd stayed strong for my kids, for Michael, but I feared music would unleash a storm inside me. I wasn't sure if I'd have the strength to gather the pieces together again.

The song grew louder. I hummed it, and suddenly I recognized it. I'd taught it the year before to our neighbor's son, a teenager who sometimes took lessons with Brendan. I hummed it again, and this time I heard the whisper of words. *I'm fifteen.*

I couldn't remember any of the other words, just that it was the song of an old man on the edge of his life, looking back through the years. He sang of his different decades, but he kept coming back to when he was fifteen, when life was filled with possibilities because he had all the time in the world. It was a pop song, not meant to be sad, but it devastated me because my son had run out of time six weeks after his fifteenth birthday.

I knelt on the floor by my bookcase, searching through the song books on the bottom shelf, tossing them aside. I flipped through songs until I finally found the sheet music. I had the title wrong. It was "100 Years," by Five for Fighting.

I took a deep breath and placed the music on the stand. My fingers fumbled as I switched on the light. I was still standing, still afraid to play, but like the night I was six, my body moved on its own. I slid onto the bench and lifted the cover. I brushed against the black-and-white keys, not making a sound, but then I gave in to my body. My arms sank deeply into the keys. I played it through, with too much pedal, my foot heavy against the pedal because I wanted each note to bleed into the next one. I played it again, singing the words, my voice raw and breathless, singing about a fifteen-year-old boy who still had time.

For weeks, I played that song and Leonard Cohen's "Hallelujah." Always alone. I couldn't breathe if anyone walked into the room. I was the mother who'd let her son die. I couldn't make another mistake. I was terrified of anyone hearing me sound anything less than perfect. I could only play for Michael and the kids, and even then, they had to stand behind me so I wouldn't see them.

When Michael told me the neighbors stood in the driveway when I sang, I closed the windows. But I couldn't stop playing. Most times, I played with my eyes closed, searching. The music flowed inside me. It pressed against my pain, making it worse. I cried with the deep bass notes stepping down. I swayed with the sixths that rolled back and forth. I rocked until I could no longer swallow my grief, and it burst out of me, a raging storm.

I was terrified I'd drown in sorrow. My mind didn't want to feel, but my body took over as if begging for the stories within the songs. I couldn't stop my fingers from playing the notes that needed to be played.

I kept playing because my body knew better than my mind. My grief was dark and heavy. It crept inside my bones until every movement was like sludging through mud. But music washed away a tiny, tiny dusting of my grief. It felt like my dreams, the ones filled with shadows and hope. It felt like water flowing over the mountains, hollowing out my heart, until slowly, a stream of light trickled within.

It was faint. Some days I couldn't feel the light, but still, I couldn't stop playing. I couldn't hold it like Michael did with his bird. I was afraid it would flow through my hands and be lost forever. I was afraid it was a mirage meant to trick me. But mostly, I was afraid I didn't deserve the light.

But still, I couldn't stop searching for it. I knew what it felt like now. This was hope. Even in the darkness, it was there. And I knew someday, somehow, I'd push through my fear and join the choir and sing with Bob and the others.

I couldn't stop playing.

27

I signed Lizzie up for the children's choir. It was only her and another little girl named Layla. The first week my mother took her, but I drove her the second week. Lizzie skipped into the sanctuary and waved goodbye before I could even talk to the choir director. I waited in the small library near the church office, looking at the titles on the bookshelf until an hour passed and the director poked her head into the room.

"There you are," she sang. "I'm Argaille." She had dark brown hair and glasses on top of her head. In the weeks before, I'd only noticed the back of her head as she played the piano. She tilted her head and smiled at me, and I almost jumped up because she looked just like Mrs. Bain.

"Isn't this such a wonderful day?" she asked, waving her arms around her. "God always makes a wonderful day. Please, come inside and I'll tell you all about our rehearsal."

I followed her down the hall, into the sanctuary. Layla and her dad sat by the piano.

"We had a great time," Argaille said. "I'm so excited Lizzie has joined our choir. Next week we'll have more children." She wiggled her fingers all around her. "Yes, Spirit will flow and we'll have more children to fill this choir."

She spread her arms wide and then clapped. "Come, Layla and

Layla's dad. Let's all gather hands in a circle. We'll go around and tell each other one thing we're grateful for. Or you can tell us one thing you're sad about. A sweet or a sour. Your choice."

I groaned silently, but reached for Lizzie's hand, hoping this would be quick. Argaille grabbed my hand. "I'll start first," she said and I marveled at the way her words seemed to gush out of her. She stared at the air for a moment and then nodded. "I'm grateful for the gift of music and the chance to work with these two beautiful girls who fill my heart with love."

Layla went next. "I'm grateful for my mom, dad and little brother." Her father nodded and said the same thing.

It was Lizzie's turn. "I'm thankful for my new puppy, Schnitzel."

Argaille threw her head back and laughed. "I love the name. Okay, Lizzie's mom. It's your turn now. A sweet or a sour."

I took a deep breath, tasting the bitterness in the back of my throat. Lizzie's sweet was still a sour for me. A week before, Michael had driven almost two hours to pick up a new puppy, a brown-and-white Shih Tzu with eyelashes so long they curled into his fur. We bought the dog to keep Lizzie company since I started teaching piano two afternoons a week. Brendan had been the one who met Lizzie at the bus stop while I was teaching. He'd ride down on his scooter and carry her backpack up the hill. We bought the puppy out of guilt, a desperate attempt to fill the hole Brendan had left behind. But of course, I couldn't say that. I closed my eyes and lied.

"I'm grateful for the mums my neighbor Kim gave me."

Argaille squeezed my hand. "Okay, everyone, that's it. See you all next week."

Layla and her dad left while Argaille packed her books into two tote bags. She talked the entire time, something about the glorious weather and Divine Spirit flowing even when it rains. She still reminded me of my piano teacher, but Mrs. Bain's movements were quiet and controlled. Argaille moved in grand gestures. She swept her arms wide and fluttered her fingers in the air, as if she played invisible keys.

"Oh, I can't keep calling you Lizzie's mom. What's your name?" she asked.

I told her. I could pinpoint the exact moment she recognized my last name. I'd thought maybe she was the pianist who had played the hymns for Brendan's funeral, but I wasn't sure until her eyes widened and she took a step back. She dropped her tote bags and flung her arms wide. "You're Brendan's mom."

I waited. Most people either looked away, not knowing what to say or their faces crumpled in sorrow. In the supermarket, some friends even swerved their carts around, pretending not to see me. I always saw them, but I let them walk away from me. I called it The Shoprite Dance.

But Argaille smiled, a wide, joyful smile that took over her whole face. She took a deep breath and then threw herself onto me. She wrapped her arms around me. I staggered back, surprised.

"I'm so happy to see you here," she said. I rolled my eyes at Lizzie and tried moving out of Argaille's hug, but she tightened her arms and rocked me. "I know he's transitioned. But dear, don't worry. He's still here."

I couldn't help but smile. *Transitioned.* I thought I'd heard all the euphemisms but this one was new. She shifted back a bit, one hand still holding mine. I could feel her vibrate. I almost expected her to twirl around in circles.

"Brendan's here," she sang and her voice echoed, floating all the way to the vaulted ceiling. "Oh, I feel him. Brendan's here." She pointed to the banner hanging on the wall behind me. It was blue with white lettering and a butterfly resting on a flower.

"All things are made new," she read slowly, enunciating each syllable. She said the words again and then gasped as if this were the first time she'd ever seen it. "All things are made new. Brendan comes in many different ways."

She looked around as if she expected to see Brendan made anew. I couldn't help but follow her gaze. She gasped again and pointed to the banner. "Look for butterflies. Always look for butterflies. Oh, do I have butterfly stories."

I sighed. I'd been hearing about butterflies since Brendan died. After Michael told everyone his bird story, friends came to me with their own magical stories of butterflies and pennies and dragonflies. I hated hearing them. Not at first. There was awe in their voices as they told me about their signs. Each time, I leaned in, feeling a spark of hope. *Yes. This will be the story that makes me believe.* But, always, they ended with a smile and I kept waiting for more. *That's it? A butterfly landed on a bush?* It wasn't nearly enough to make me believe.

I pulled back from Argaille, not wanting to hear her own story about a butterfly. She dropped her hands by her side, her eyes still wide as she let out a long sigh. "Brendan's here. I'm so blessed I could share this with you." She smiled at Lizzie. "She told me you play the piano. Please, play something for me."

I looked at the piano. I had spent the afternoon playing a Chopin Nocturne. The left hand notes were a sea of triplets, tiny waves that moved through me as I played. It should have been so easy to slide onto the bench and share the song with her. But fear slammed into me, the same fear that stopped me from playing in front of others.

I shook my head. "I can't. I have injuries." There was nothing to see in my arm, but I held it up, my arm shaking, offering proof that it was an injury stopping me from playing. Argaille nodded. "Of course."

"Maybe soon," Lizzie said as we walked away. She slipped her arm into mine and I smiled down at her. I did have a slew of injuries. Carpal tunnel had settled in my wrists years ago. A constant ache lived in my left thumb and elbow. I'd learned to push through the pain.

It wasn't an injury that made my arm tremble. It was fear.

28

I sat on the front steps while Zack and Lizzie played with Schnitzel, our new puppy, under the maple tree. Its leaves were beginning to turn red and orange. Snowbelle was inside the house, since Schnitzel liked to jump on her and bite her ears. Zack tossed a yarn ball at Schnitzel, but he ignored it and stretched out on the grass, the afternoon sun warming his belly. Zack gave up and curled next to him, sliding him into the crook of his body. Lizzie kept trying to pet him, but Zack blocked her hand. "Back off. It's my turn now."

I looked at the clock on my phone. "Only another minute. Then it's Lizzie's turn."

"You know what?" Zack sat up. "I just realized something. Brendan's named both dogs. He was the one who named Snowbelle. And in a way, he named Schnitzel."

Ten years ago, Michael had carried home a tiny puppy with white pillowy hair. "She looks like a snowball," Brendan said, his face buried in her fur. "But we can't name her that. We need to be original. We'll call her Snowbelle. With an E at the end. No one would think of that."

The new puppy was named after Brendan's obsession for the schnitzel he'd tasted from a food truck. One bite of the salty, crunchy breaded cutlet, and he was hooked.

"I'm going to write that in the memory book," Zack said and scooped up Schnitzel, placing him in Lizzie's lap. He ran inside. I kept the notebook on the counter for everyone to see and write in, still so afraid of losing our memories of Brendan. I wrote about his silly walks, inspired by a Monty Python skit his Uncle Jim had shown him. Lizzie wrote about the time they went to the park together, riding bikes until the ice cream truck came. Every few days, we remembered something new, but this was the first time Zack had written a memory down.

"Daddy's home," Lizzie yelled. Schnitzel started barking. Michael pulled into the driveway but didn't get out right away. I thought he was on the phone with work, but then he jerked his head back, laughing. He slammed his hands into the steering wheel. I sighed. *Another song.*

It made no sense to me that Brendan was sending him songs. There was part of me that wanted to give into the flow, but always, I resisted. There were even days I wanted to squash his faith, to burst that electric energy that seemed to dance around him. But I couldn't.

Michael opened the car door and jumped out. "Another song," he yelled. He held up his phone. He always googled the lyrics once he heard a song in the car. " It's "Have a Little Faith in Me." By John Hiatt. Check it out."

He shoved the phone in my hand. I squinted at the lyrics, trying to see what Michael felt.

"See?" He pointed to the screen. "It's about being in the dark, but love always being there. Even when you can't see, love is there. You have to have a little faith. I asked Brendan to help me believe. And this is what he sent me."

The songs Brendan had sent him had grown over the past few weeks. We'd kept Brendan's phone and each night Michael fell asleep listening to one of his playlists. Sometimes, I'd get caught up in his excitement and try to read something into the songs. Some of the lyrics touched me. But mostly, I wondered how Michael thought Brendan controlled the airwaves. I asked him that once.

"I don't know," he'd said with a shrug. "I don't understand how music travels through the air into my car, but I still listen to it. It's the same thing with Brendan. I don't understand it, not even a little. But it doesn't matter. Not when it fills me with this feeling."

He smiled at Zack when he came back outside.

"Look, I got another song." Michael held up the phone, but Zack barely glanced at it. "Cool," he said and skipped down the stairs, ready to claim his time with Schnitzel. Lizzie didn't even look up. Zack and Lizzie had loved the songs. They used to crowd around Michael, staring at his scrap of paper and then the lyrics, as if Brendan had texted them from worlds away. But now? The songs were an everyday wonder for them.

Michael pressed play on the song and sat down next to me on the stairs. We listened while watching the kids chase Schnitzel around the front yard. I leaned back on my elbows. Michael had his eyes closed, a dreamy smile on his face.

"What do you feel when Brendan touches you?" I asked softly.

He opened his eyes and his smile widened. "It's magic," he whispered. "It's hard to explain, hard to put it into words. That's why I love the songs. They say what I can't say."

"But what do you feel?"

He looked at me. "It's like pins and needles."

"Where do you feel it?"

"In my shoulders. Down my back. But it's more than pins and needles. It's almost like a cold sensation, like water running through me."

"Is that why you shiver?" I'd felt something like that the day we were on the trail when the woman shouted about heaven. And maybe a tiny bit in the dreams I had. But it quickly went away. I wanted more. Needed more. I leaned forward, searching for his formula to feel our son.

He shook his head. "No, that's the weird thing. It's cold and yet it makes me feel warm. It's an incredible feeling."

He stilled and then shivered, a long slow one that seemed to move through his whole body. "He's here," he whispered. "I'm feeling him right now."

I stared at the air around him, trying to see what he felt.

"Oh, Linda, if you could only feel this," he said. He stretched out his hand. "Take my hand. I think he's holding my hand right now. Take it. Then you'll feel him. Take it," he said when I only stared at him. "Take it."

The song, set on loop, started again. *Have a little faith.* Slowly, I reached out and wrapped my fingers around his. I closed my eyes.

"That's it," he whispered. "Don't think. Just feel."

I tried. I felt the chill of the concrete steps seep into my thighs. I felt his ring bite into my finger as he tried squeezing Brendan into me. I felt the wind whisper through my hair. But Brendan? No.

My family never talked about feeling my sister around us; we barely talked about her at all. I filled the void by sneaking into my mother's closet and pulling out her cardboard box filled with Elizabeth's medical records. I wrote down words I didn't know and biked to the library to research them. I needed facts. That's how I built my wall. I pieced myself back together, fact by fact.

"Feel," Michael said, his voice growing louder. "It's getting stronger." He stood up, yanking me to my feet, holding both of my hands. "Wow, it's so strong. Can you feel him?"

I closed my eyes and tried one more time. Nothing. I shook my head. I broke free and turned toward the door. "I need to go inside now and start dinner."

"Wait." He reached out and held my arm. "I'm sorry. I really thought—" He dropped his hand. "It's just that he's so strong. I thought for sure you would feel him."

I stared at him, waiting for more, but he had nothing left to say.

29

At the end of September, Rev. Rick pulled Michael and me aside before the service. "I'd like to officially welcome you to church today," he said.

I couldn't say no to that. I thought he'd have us stand, and he'd say a few words, and then we'd smile and nod at the people who still brought us meals. We'd sit back down, and I'd resume staring at the wooden cross hanging from the ceiling. It hurt to look at it, a reminder of the casket that was once under it, but I couldn't stop seeking out this pain. It was like a toothache my tongue kept probing, testing to see if the pain still stabbed at me.

After we stood for the final prayer, Rev. Rick pointed to us. "They've been coming here for a few weeks, so today, I'd like to officially welcome the Broders to our church."

Lizzie had slept over at a friend's house so it was only Zack in between Michael and me. Faces turned, smiling as they welcomed us. "As you know," he continued, "they joined our church under tragic circumstances."

Zack's fists clenched. I wanted to put my arm around him, but he was tight, his body brittle. I was afraid he'd run from the church. I was afraid I'd follow him and never return.

"They lost their teenage son in an accident. He was fifteen. Losing a child—" his voice broke and he stopped for a moment. I tightened my jaw so the sob inside me couldn't escape. I couldn't stop the tears flowing from my eyes. I grabbed the pack of tissues someone had left in the pew.

"I want them to know we are here to help. UPC will help them through this tragedy."

He continued to talk, but I missed some of what he was saying. I was focused on Zack. His whole body shook. I leaned down to whisper something to him. Before I could, a hand from behind fell on my shoulder. It was meant for comfort, but, still I flinched and inched away. Another hand trapped me underneath its weight. I didn't turn; I didn't even know whose hand it was.

Why are they touching me?

"We will pray with you," Rev. Rick said, his voice cutting through the panic inside my head.

I bit my lip, feeling the weight of yet another hand. Three hands were on me now. My knees buckled. I moved forward, twisting, pretending to reach for another tissue, anything to escape the weight on my shoulders and back, but they stretched with me, holding on.

I looked over at Michael. *Let's get the hell out of here,* my eyes screamed. He didn't understand, though. Hands were on his back and shoulders. They didn't drag him down; with each weight, he stood taller.

One settled on Zack and then another. He didn't wrench away either. He unfurled his clenched fists, his fingers fumbling for mine and then Michael's. He squeezed hard. The couple in front of us turned around, both reaching for his shoulder. Tears dripped down his face but his trembling eased.

I looked around. It wasn't just those around us holding on. People flowed into the aisles, stretching out and leaning forward, until hands fell on top of hands. When there was no more room to reach us, one person reached out for another, holding on, until we became an unbroken chain that led back to Rev. Rick.

I would have said no if I'd known what welcoming us meant. I didn't know I'd feel the weight of all these hands crushing me.

"We will pray with you," he said again. "But when you can't look up to God, when the pain is too great and you are filled with anger, that's okay. You don't need to pray."

As one, everyone nodded, giving me permission not to pray. His words flowed through our connected hands. Except for that last Tuesday in August, I hadn't prayed to God since the priest had been in my house when I was fourteen.

You don't need to pray, the Rev had just said. *You can be filled with anger toward God.* The hands still held onto me, but the weight felt lighter now.

"We will pray with you," he continued. "But when you can't, we will pray for you."

The church nodded and their murmurs swept over me, weaving inside me like the web they'd made with their hands. I'd known already that people prayed for us. But this was different. This church, this community, would hold the prayers I couldn't whisper. They'd carry them up to God. I didn't have to pray. They would do it for me.

These strangers would hold my faith for me. Hands covered my back and my shoulders, but they no longer pushed me down. Tears blurred my eyes. I reached across Zack with my other hand and held onto Michael and knew he felt the connection of not just the three of us, but the entire church who shared our pain and cried with us as their hands wove a web big enough to build a bridge. I wasn't sure when I'd be able to cross this river of pain. I wasn't sure if I'd ever be able to pray again. But I knew this bridge, built by the hands of believers, would be waiting for me.

This church, these strangers would pray for me. They didn't care that I burned with rage. That right now, I didn't believe in God's goodness or his mercy. There were times when I didn't believe in God at all. Still, they stood around us, offering us strength and faith.

They held my faith, cupped gently within their hands, waiting until I could claim it for myself. I didn't need to think. I could just let go and feel.

A small part of me opened up, enough for another sliver of light to slip in. I wasn't sure what to believe in anymore. Could I believe in the birds that knocked on my door or the songs Michael wrote down? Or the bird that sat hidden at the bottom of my tote bag? Or this church that held my faith for me?

It was like a rope and, for once, I wasn't afraid to reach out and grab hold of it.

I wanted the light. I wanted to lean into those hands woven together. They didn't care what I believed in. They kept shining the light. For the first time since Brendan died, I let myself feel the power of faith.

I touched the light and believed in hope.

30

In October, I found the second wooden bird. A large armoire occupied our front hallway. I'd stared at it for days, hating how big it was. It seemed to loom over me when I walked in the door, like a shadow that covered me in darkness. I had to move it.

Michael dragged it off to the garage so we could place a dresser there instead. I grabbed a broom, but then saw another blue wooden bird on the floor. It was covered by dust, yet it seemed to glow.

I brushed away the dirt. Michael was still in the garage. I didn't want him seeing it, didn't want him making a fuss, but I couldn't stop myself from pulling out the first bird from my bag. I held the two of them in my cupped hand for a long time. They seemed to float and, for a moment, I felt electric wonder dance around me. I couldn't move when the garage door rattled open, not even when Michael walked up behind me and spotted the birds.

I shrugged. "I've been finding them in the house. This is the second one."

Michael nudged one of the birds with his finger. "Wow," he said. There was too much awe in his voice. It overwhelmed me. "It's Brendan. He's leaving them for you to find."

I snapped my hand into a fist. I'd felt something, a tiny bit of magic. I could almost believe that somehow Brendan had touched me, had whispered in my ear. *Reach into the bottom of your bag.*

Move the dresser. Maybe he was helping me find the birds, something I didn't even know I'd lost.

But the idea that he was *leaving them* for me to find was too much. It washed away any trace of magic and logic won out. I laughed at Michael, dismissing his words.

I pointed to the dresser. "Let's move it now." I spent the afternoon decorating the front hallway, trying to make it seem warm and welcoming when Zack and Lizzie walked into the house. I wanted them to believe that everything was fine.

We didn't talk about the wooden birds again. I couldn't throw them away, though. When he wasn't looking, I dropped the birds back into my bag. I made myself a rule that I couldn't reach inside to hold them. I could only touch them through the fabric. But each time I left the house, I loved knowing that I carried them with me.

The two wooden birds I'd found made Michael bold. He tied a bird feeder onto the tree we'd planted the month before Brendan was born. He hung another in the backyard and bought bags of birdseed, giant bags I couldn't even lift. He filled them each Saturday, after Zack had mowed the lawn.

It was Zack who'd asked to take over Brendan's job of mowing. At first, I couldn't watch while Michael was teaching him, afraid I'd only see that day when Brendan bent over the mower for the first time, Michael by his side. But I didn't want to lose a Zack memory either. I stood on the front steps, smiling at Zack standing behind the lawn mower. I saw him at three, his blond hair dipping into his eyes, slipping a plastic hammer into his overalls, following Michael into the garage. "Me too, me too," he yelled and pounded pretend nails into wood.

I saw Zack at four, carrying up his plastic lawn mower from the basement. He walked behind Michael as he cut the grass, his mower spraying bubbles into the air. "Me too," he said as he followed the path Michael made. Even at four, he insisted that one day he'd join the family business Papa Ben had started. He'd slip on one of Michael's BHB shirts and scribble on service report slips.

I watched Zack now, at thirteen, his hair darkened to brown. He wore the same Yankee baseball cap as Michael. He chewed on his lips as he pushed the mower, his arms straining. He wasn't as strong as Brendan had been at fifteen, but he was determined. Sweat dripped into his eyes, and his cheeks flushed, but he didn't give up. He no longer shouted, "Me too," but his body still yelled the words. When he was done mowing, he picked up the bag of birdseed, hauling it over his shoulder, just like he'd seen his dad do. His knees buckled under the weight.

"I can do it," he said when Michael moved to help him. "I can do it." He walked down the steps to the backyard, spilling a trail of seeds.

Michael walked over to me and raised his eyebrows. "Do you see them?" Black birds were scattered across the grass, pecking at the seeds on the ground. A few sparrows fluttered by the feeder and even more birds I didn't recognize sat on the branches, waiting their turn. "I told you they'd come," he said.

"Of course they're coming," I said. "You put out birdseed. That's what birds do. They come for the seed."

Michael shrugged. "They came first, before I even put out a single seed. But does it matter? They're still here."

It wasn't complicated for Michael. He believed Brendan sent him messages in birds and songs. He didn't worry about logic or rules the way I did. I was so careful with my words, so very careful.

So was Brendan. When he was six, he sat at the kitchen table making a birthday card for his best friend Dylan. I showed him how to sign it—"Love, Brendan." He tilted his head, staring down at the words. "He's my best friend, but do I love him?" He chewed on his pencil and thought about it for minutes. In the end, he signed it "Your friend" because he wasn't completely sure it was love. He didn't want to write something that might not be true.

That's how I felt, staring at the birds Michael had invited, afraid to believe in something that might not be true.

"And what if you're wrong?" I asked. What if I believed Brendan put a bird in my bag, and then I found out it was one of my students who'd snuck it inside. I wanted to hold onto a tiny dusting of magic, but I was afraid if I learned the truth, it would wash away everything. The sparrow tapping on my door. The woman yelling heaven on the trail. The songs Michael put into Brendan's playlists.

"What if you're wrong?" I asked again.

He shrugged. "If I'm wrong, I'll still be grateful because it made me think of Brendan."

I shook my head. "You're such a simple man."

He laughed, knowing I didn't mean it as an insult. I wished I had his faith, to feel that magic, but logic stood in my way.

"A simple, simple man," I said as I went into the house, wishing I could throw away my rules. I had so many of them, even for the way I could grieve.

In those early weeks, I'd crawled into Brendan's bed, pretending I could still feel his warmth. I did it for hours each day, so I made myself a rule that I could only do it once a week. And when I couldn't follow my own rule, I took apart his bed so I'd no longer be tempted.

I wanted to be like Michael. Simple. Living in the moment, like a child. I wanted to pull my birds out of the bag and set them on a pedestal. I wanted to shine a light on them. That's what Michael would do. But I couldn't.

I was the one who kept birds hidden in the bottom of my bag.

31

Lizzie and Zack sat at the kitchen counter doing homework. The dogs were under their chairs, hoping for a scrap of their apples and cheese. My iPad was on the counter playing the song "Have a Little Faith in Me." I still didn't believe Brendan was sending them, but I listened to them anyway. The sun was beginning to set; I'd already turned on the lights so I could chase away the shadows.

I was about to slip a tray of stuffed peppers into the oven but stopped when Michael ran into the house and yelled. "I have a new one," he shouted and the dogs barked at his feet. I could barely hear the music from the iPad over the noise.

"This one," he said, slapping the paper onto the table. "This one will make you believe." I held my breath. A little ribbon of hope curled inside me. He seemed so sure. He pointed to the paper, his finger shaking. "Look," he said, but I couldn't read his scribble.

"I was at the cemetery," he said, "asking Brendan for a sign he was all right. And then I turned on my car. And guess what came on right away? "Knockin' on Heaven's Door." Don't you see? I was asking him if he was all right and he answered. He's in heaven."

Lizzie jumped up, clapping her hands. Zack looked up from his textbook and smiled. I nodded, hoping that was enough for Michael, but he held his hands out wide, waiting for me to burst with belief.

But I didn't want to believe in something that could be taken away.

I'd fought sleep in the weeks after Brendan died. It took every ounce of my strength to hold myself together. I was terrified I'd wake in the morning, and in those hazy first seconds, I'd forget what happened. I'd think it was just a nightmare and maybe for a few minutes, we'd be a family of five. Then reality would slam into me and I'd shatter all over again. I wasn't sure if I could piece myself together again.

I couldn't take the risk. I couldn't believe in the birds that sang to me each day or the songs Michael brought home. There were days I couldn't even touch the wooden birds hidden in my bag. Instead I stared at sand.

On our last vacation in Cape May, we'd bought a wooden picture frame filled with blue shades of sand suspended in liquid. Each time the frame was flipped, sand dripped down, forming an abstract picture. I kept it on the windowsill by the stairs so sunlight could shine through it.

It seemed harmless, a vacation memento meant to be displayed. But after Brendan died, I saw so much more in it. I turned over the frame and watched sand drip in tiny streams. Twenty minutes later, I searched the final picture, mining it for meaning. I saw birds and once, a profile that looked like him. I even took a picture of it. I only allowed myself to do it once a day. It was silly, and yet it was safer for me to stand on the stairs and watch sand trickle down, searching the shapes for something I could believe in.

So I shook my head when Michael pointed to the scrap of paper. I turned away. I didn't want to see the word he'd written down. *Heaven.*

"It's time to put your books away," I said to Zack and Lizzie. "It's almost time for dinner." But before anyone moved, my iPad stopped mid-song, and the screen went blank. I thought the battery had died, but then the screen flashed on and off and then on again. I frowned.

The iPad started scrolling through songs, still flickering. No one touched it, and yet it jumped from playlist to playlist as if it were searching for a song.

It stopped. A new song started playing, a song that wasn't even on the playlist. I looked over at Michael. His grin grew wider. The opening chords of "Knockin' on Heaven's Door" filled the room. He held up his hands. "I didn't touch it. No one did. It did it all on its own."

Bob Dylan started singing about heaven. Michael reached for my hands. This time, I felt something. A little spark between our palms. I stared down at our hands as if I could see it crackle with electricity. "You have to believe," he said. "It's Brendan."

Lizzie jumped up, and Zack closed his book. It was the first time they were there for a sign, not just hearing Michael speak about it. The four of us said nothing as we listened to the song. Michael kept nodding as if Brendan were speaking to him right there in the room. When the song ended, the iPad stopped, and we stood there in the quiet staring at each other. I took a breath and then another. I looked at Michael and smiled. The kids watched me. Waiting. Finally, I broke the silence.

"Yes," I whispered. "Yes."

Michael squeezed my hands. Lizzie shouted, "Hooray!" I laughed and said it again. "Yes." My voice grew louder with each one. "Yes. Yes. Yes!"

The kids danced around the kitchen, the dogs barking at their feet. It was no longer just the four of us. At that moment, we were a family of five. Michael whirled me around, and I threw my head back, feeling a current of wonder move through me. Perhaps it was the madness of grief slipping inside me. I didn't care. It felt so good.

For three minutes and ten seconds, I believed. I believed.

*

After dinner, I walked into our bedroom, still humming the song. Michael sat on the edge of the bed, looking down at something in his hand. I recognized the business card; it wasn't a song. He looked up, his eyes hopeful. He shrugged, asking an unspoken question.

I'd laughed the first time Michael asked to go to a medium. It was the second day of school for Zack and Lizzie. He'd been out walking Snowy, waiting until the sun had set and our street was wrapped in night. He kept his head down, not wanting to talk to anyone. But Anna must have seen him. She handed him a card. Friends had given us numbers of psychiatrists and support groups, but never one for a medium.

He walked into the house holding the phone number high just like the slips of paper containing song titles. I pretended not to see the way he traced the medium's name with his finger. I treated it like a joke. I laughed and tossed the card into the garbage.

He must have taken it out. He looked at me now, waiting for an answer. I shook my head.

He blew out his breath in frustration. "I don't understand. You felt Brendan before. I know you did. And you feel him when you play the piano. And when you pick up rocks? You pick up so many, putting them back until you find the one that feels like Brendan. Don't you want more of that?"

Of course I did. Every part of me yearned to feel him more. I had a rock in my pocket right now.

Michael held up the card, as if that would change my mind. "Anna goes at least once a year. Her grandfather comes through and sometimes her mother. Rhonda is the medium. She says things she couldn't possibly know. Like how her grandfather would tap people with his cane. How could she have known that?"

I shrugged. "These mediums know exactly how to prey on grieving people. They know what to look for and what to say to make you believe."

We'd only spoken of a medium once before, after his sister Trudy visited one. I dismissed it as entertainment, like a séance at a slumber party. I thought Michael had laughed with me at the time, but his face was serious now. "I believe in mediums. Do you?" he asked.

"Maybe. I'm not sure." A few months ago, I would have said no without hesitation. But I wasn't so sure now. Not after today. I sat down next to him on the bed and shrugged. "I think so."

"That's the problem. You're thinking too much. You know that gets you into trouble. You need to just feel. And stop thinking." He nudged me with his elbow. "Remember the time we went running?"

I'd tried running with him years ago. The first few yards were fine, but then I kept turning to him, asking questions. Where do my arms go? Do I land on my toes? Do I time my breath with my feet? His own movements grew jerky. Finally, he stumbled to a stop, forgetting for a second how to run. "Just run," he said. "Don't think. Just feel."

He said it again now. *Just feel.* I tried to feel myself into belief. But so many questions ran through my mind. "It doesn't matter," I said. "Even if I did believe in some mediums, most of them are con artists."

A few hours ago, I'd felt Brendan. I knew he was there. But now Michael wanted me to visit a stranger, someone who only wanted money from me.

How could I believe in that?

After Michael fell asleep, I slipped out of bed and went downstairs to my laptop. I couldn't sleep. Her name kept running through my head. *Rhonda Silvers. Medium.* I googled her and clicked on her website. There was a picture of her in the middle of the page. She had long dark hair and a pretty smile. *Just an ordinary woman.* I'd expected a turban and beads draped down to her waist and a long dress that flowed around her.

She claimed she was a psychic and a medium. I didn't even know there was a difference. I researched the terms. A medium spoke to the dead while a psychic could see the future. I shuddered, hating the idea that the future could be predicted. I scrolled down and looked at her rates. Two hundred dollars for a session. It wasn't cheap. I snorted when I saw she had emergency rates for when a family really needed to get in contact with a loved one.

What a scam.

I scrolled back up. I laughed when I saw the butterfly on her page.

Of course. Another damn butterfly.

32

Lizzie loved the sympathy cards. They came almost every day, even six weeks later. She skipped to the mailbox and carried an armful of cards into the house. It was her way of talking about Brendan, of trying to make sense of his death.

She'd sit at the kitchen table, slide her finger under the flap of the envelope and pull out the card slowly, holding it to her heart for a moment. She opened each card with a long sigh, believing in the words of comfort written in silvery script. Her favorite one had pastel flowers scattered across the card. "Look, Mommy," she said. "Your tears are watering the garden of memories."

I used that line often. I didn't want to scare her and Zack. I only let them see the gentle tears meant for a Hallmark card. "Just watering the garden," I'd say, wiping away any evidence of sadness. My real tears came each night when Michael came home and I could escape the house and stand in the middle of the street and stare at the stars.

One night, I slipped out of the house and stood on my front steps. I ran my hands over the orange and yellow silk leaves I'd threaded through the railing. I shifted the pumpkin on the steps, tilting it at the perfect angle next to the bucket of apples and the bales of hay I'd hauled from the farm around the corner. The front steps needed light and maybe a scarecrow, but it was enough to fool my friends.

"That's how I knew you were okay," a friend said. "You decorated your house for fall."

I didn't tell her I'd spent most of that morning counting. That I woke up knowing it had been forty-seven days since my son died, but I needed to know the hours, the minutes, the seconds. I spent the morning staring at numbers.

That night, I walked to the end of my driveway where the trees no longer blocked the stars. I'd spent nights staring at the stars and still, I couldn't recognize them. Michael showed me a sky chart, but even when I found one glittering in the sky, I couldn't trace the lines that connected its constellation. His sister Trudy had registered a star in Brendan's name, but I could never find him.

Still, the stars pulled me out each night, a magnet that dragged me, even when they hid behind the clouds. They seemed to speak to me, begging me to cry underneath their light. I was about to step into the middle of the street when I heard the front door open. Lizzie stood on the porch, shrugging into a sweatshirt. She walked down the steps. I slipped on my mask of a gentle smile, inhaling patience with a silent breath.

I didn't want her here. I'd done my job for today. I'd stumbled out of bed with the whine of the school bus turning into our development. I met my daughter at the bottom of the hill and carried her backpack as she chattered on about the mysteries of the fifth grade lunch table. I ran in circles with Zack, chasing the dogs in the backyard and not once, not even once did I stop and look at the darkened window of an empty room. I stayed strong and did my job.

"Go inside, sweetie," I said. "I just need a few minutes."

She shook her head and kept walking. "I want to stay with you."

I wanted her to go inside and snuggle next to Michael. It was his turn for fake smiles and the jokes he'd practiced on the train ride home. I told her again to go inside, but again she shook her head. I bit the inside of my cheek, trying to hold back my tears. They wouldn't be the gentle ones I allowed myself in front of the kids. I waved toward the front door, but she only moved closer until she stood next to me. I took a deep breath.

Finally, I whispered, "Mommy needs to cry."

I wanted her to run inside and crawl into safety, but she smiled. "It's okay." She slipped her hand into mine and held on tight. "I want to cry with you."

Lizzie smiled again, her eyes already filling, waiting for me to allow the tears to come. I tried to be strong, but my control shattered, and raw, broken sobs burst out. She said nothing, only squeezed my hand tighter and cried with me. I didn't try to stop the tears or worry if they were too much for her. We stood together and cried, only it was so much more than tears. They were howls that echoed in the night.

We cried until we gasped for air, until our sobs faded into whimpers. We grew silent and for a few minutes, we listened to the wind rustling the last leaves clinging to their branches. It seemed almost peaceful. And then she burped, a loud one that made us both giggle.

She pointed to a star, a bright, shimmering one. "Maybe that's Brendan."

I nodded. The star was ancient, formed from clouds of dust billions of years ago, but still, I searched the sky each night, wondering which one was him.

She sighed. "I miss him." She pointed to a spot on the driveway. "He used to stand there every morning and wait until I looked out the window. Then he'd give me a silly wave. A different one for each day. And when I was sick, he always let me cuddle with him."

I froze. Oh, how I wanted to talk about Brendan. Sometimes, I stood alone in the kitchen and whispered his name. I needed to hear his name, but when Zack and Lizzie came home from school, I was so afraid of crying and losing control in front of them that I couldn't say his name. Instead we talked about basketball and Girl Scouts and the meals the neighbors brought. But that night, standing with Lizzie, I'd been emptied of tears and the memories of Brendan rushed in.

I smiled, picturing the way he made room for her in his bed or on the couch. "He always tucked a blanket around you when you were sick."

"Yes," Lizzie said, clapping her hands and jumping up and down. "Once, he put all the blankets in the house on me. I think I had ten of them! I could barely move." She laughed, her hands wrapped around her middle. She looked up. Her eyes widened. "When I laugh holding my belly like that, it sounds like Brendan."

She laughed again, and I closed my eyes, listening to the sound of Brendan. I needed more. I told her about the time he had a nosebleed in class. He was afraid his teacher would see the smudges of blood on his hand and didn't want to be sent to the nurse. Before she could notice, he grabbed a red marker and colored all over his hands to hide the evidence.

He hated being fussed over when he was hurt. One time, I had come home and found a trail of blood and Band-aid wrappers leading into the den. He was sitting on his hand, hiding his injury. He'd twisted the Band-aid around his finger so tight, its tip had turned purple.

She told me about the times late at night when he scrambled eggs, standing at the stove in his underwear. Sometimes, he tiptoed into her room and shook her shoulder, waking her up so she could taste the most perfect plate of eggs.

"One day I'm not going to wear anything at all when I make my eggs," he told her. "Naked at the stove at midnight, stirring my eggs and scratching my butt. That's my dream."

Lizzie and I laughed until our ribs ached. I loved hearing about their secret world. Then we turned back to the stars, wondering where he was.

"Stars can sing," I told her. I'd read that when I was trying to learn about constellations.

"Really? How?"

I shrugged. "I don't know, but scientists discovered sound waves coming from them, like a hum. It's so low we can't hear it. They can even measure their frequency, just like musical notes. It's a symphony of stars."

"Singing stars." She laughed and then ran for the front door. "I'm going to tell Daddy and Zack."

I stayed outside for a few minutes more, staring up at the stars singing to each other. I couldn't hear their songs, but sometimes, I imagined I felt them, a low hum echoing in my heart. Maybe this was why the stars pulled me outside each night. They shimmered like the stories of Brendan, the ones I'd kept locked deep inside, afraid to unleash an avalanche of pain. But crying with Lizzie broke through that. We shared his stories until they began to shine, like a hum swelling into a song.

His death had torn something inside me, a ragged hole that seemed impossible to fill. But these stories, oh, I knew now, his stories could somehow knit me back together.

The stories would sometimes come with tears. That's why I'd pushed them away. I thought I needed to be strong, to show my kids strength and resolve, and not let them see me broken. That was my job as a mother, to soothe them, pick them up and kiss their skinned knees and silence their tears.

I'd watched my mother push away the pain. The night after my sister's funeral, I'd walked into my room and found my mother sitting in the dark inside Elizabeth's closet, tears streaming down her face. She didn't hear me, never even looked up. I backed away before she could.

But Lizzie had seen my tears. She didn't back away, not even when I begged. She moved toward me. I didn't know that was an option when I was little. That I could crawl inside the darkness with my mother, and together we'd cry.

I'd learned how to be strong for others. But maybe, there was another way? Something my ten-year-old daughter taught me. Being strong didn't mean I couldn't feel my sorrow. I could let Zack and Lizzie see me fall down, as long as they watched me get back up again. I could let them see my pain, as long as they also saw me doubled over with laughter. I didn't always need to put on a smile and hide my tears.

Under a sky filled with stars, I could let them see me cry.

33

Despite Argaille's constant affirmation that new kids would show up the following week, there were only a few students in the children's choir. Most of the time it was just Lizzie and Layla.

One day, Layla hadn't arrived yet, so Argaille welcomed Lizzie into the sanctuary with a sweep of her hand. I shook my head when she included me in that wave. Each week, she'd invite me to play her something and I'd freeze, terrified of even pressing one key.

"I have injuries," I'd remind her and she'd bow her head.

"Of course," she said, but there was something in her voice, something in the way she tilted her head. She spoke of me singing with the choir, even talked about the music as if I were the one who'd asked to join. I kept shaking my head, but she didn't seem to notice.

I stayed in the narthex that day, the room next to the sanctuary, listening to Lizzie warm up. Her voice echoed in the empty room and carried through the open doors. When Layla still hadn't arrived, Argaille asked Lizzie about her day.

"I'm trying out for show choir at school."

"That's wonderful, dear. What song are you singing?"

"Wake Me Up When September Ends." She'd chosen the Green Day song in early August, weeks before anything happened. I flinched each time I heard the words, but Lizzie never noticed. She sang, her voice filling the room. I was surprised she could sing by herself so easily. She showed no hesitation, no fear.

Why can't I do that?

I listened to Lizzie sing while I paced around the narthex. I stopped in front of the stained-glass window. I'd never noticed it before; it was almost hidden, wrapped in the shadows. The sun was setting; its colors were dull and muted. That's how I felt, trapped in the darkness. I yearned for the light.

I traced around the glass, my fingers trembling. For a moment, I wished I were in a Catholic church where I could slip my money into the metal holder and light a candle. I'd watch the wick burst into light and kneel before the flickering flame and pray for something, the way I stood in the hospital room and prayed for God to save my son. I hadn't prayed since that day. But now I wanted to pray for courage to join the choir.

But I couldn't pray to God. Instead, I turned to Brendan. I talked with him all the time. But I was afraid to ask him to help me. Partly, because it seemed strange as his mother to be the one to ask for help. But I was also terrified to lose that flame flickering inside me these past few weeks. Hope had stirred inside me that day in church when I'd felt those hands resting on me. Even more whenever I heard the song "Knockin' on Heaven's Door." I was terrified to test that feeling, to ask for something I could never have, but the shadows darkening the stained-glass window scared me more. I clasped my hands together.

Please, Brendan. Give me courage.

It was my first request for Brendan. A simple one. I didn't ask for a miracle; I didn't even ask for him to visit me in my dreams like he did for Michael. I asked to sing with Bob and the church choir; one small step that still made me shake as I stood there, begging Brendan to give me courage.

Later that night after we'd finished dinner and the kids ran up to do homework, I told Michael how I'd asked Brendan for the courage to join the choir. I knew he'd be excited, but I didn't expect him to jump up.

"Oh, my God. That's what it means."

He ran over to the phone where he kept his wallet and leafed through the scraps of paper. "Today, after I left the bank, a song came on the radio. It's a SONG."

He drew out the word, said it as if each letter were capitalized, as if I could see the word sparkle in the air between us.

"Linda." He stopped and took a breath. "As soon as I heard it, I got this feeling. Brendan gave me this song, only I didn't understand it. Now I know the song was for you. I wrote it down." He handed me the slip of paper. "It's for you. He heard you and gave me your song."

I held the paper in my palm. I'd said yes to "Knockin' on Heaven's Door." I'd said yes to the wooden birds still in my bag. But this was the first time I'd asked Brendan for something, the first time I'd asked him to prove he was still around me. My hand shook.

"You need to believe in him," Michael said. "Believe in our son."

I unfurled my fingers and looked down at the title he'd written on the paper.

Courage.

"Don't you see?" Michael asked. "The song he gave me was "Courage." I didn't know what he was trying to tell me, but now I know. He's giving you courage to join the choir."

Tears pricked my eyes. I tried to hold onto the logistics of Brendan sending him a song that was exactly what I had asked for, but I couldn't, not when I was looking at the word *Courage*. "Do you really think so?"

He smiled. "What time were you at Lizzie's choir?"

"Around five."

"Exactly." He pointed to the paper. "Look at the time stamp from the bank. Five-fifteen. He heard you and sent me this song. He's giving you courage, Linda. Your son is giving you courage."

I looked at Michael. *I want to believe. I want to hold onto this and never let go.*

Is that enough for faith? The desire to believe? Could I grab hold of this tiny piece of paper, desperate to believe Brendan wanted me to sing with others?

Courage.

I wasn't sure if this was faith, but for now, it seemed like enough for me to push through my fear and join the choir.

An hour later, Argaille called. Like a hawk zeroing in on its prey, she somehow sensed my interest and wasn't about to let me go. The phone rang when we were cleaning up the kitchen.

"Linda," she shouted into the phone. "Dear, it's Argaille. From UPC." I moved the phone away from my ear. Argaille rushed on, not waiting for me to respond, "And so, I wanted to dive right in and throw this out to the universe."

I frowned, trying to figure out her words.

"This is right. The universe is always right," she said. "This is Divine Flow."

"I'm not sure I'm following. What's right?"

She laughed. "Yes, of course, I did forget to say that. You joining the choir. Now, I made you a folder with music. It's in the choir room. For you to look at whenever you're ready. Oh, can't you feel the flow moving all around us?"

My breath stopped for a second. I wanted to take it slow, think about it for a few weeks. I needed a ten-step plan for joining a choir. Maybe this weekend I'd sing with the windows open. Or with Zack and Lizzie in the room where I could see them. Baby steps.

"There's no pressure," Argaille said. I almost laughed over that. She'd already made me a folder. Called me at home. I was afraid to imagine what she'd think was pressure.

"Look over the music this weekend and see if anything moves you." She spoke like music, her sentences filled with dramatic contrasts of loud and soft. She varied her tempos and added accented words that always managed to startle me.

"Let the *Spirit* wash over you and *guide* you into choosing what's right. It's a flow, dear. A wonderful mystical flow."

How could I respond to that? Still feeling the high from before, I mumbled something about seeing her next week. Argaille took it as a yes.

"Then it's settled," she said. There was a moment when I could have said no, but I didn't. Argaille hung up before I could change my mind.

I stared at the phone for a minute, my hands still shaking.

"What was that all about?" Michael asked.

I shrugged. "I guess I'm going to let the spirit wash over me."

He smirked. "Dare I ask what that means? And does it involve a ceremony of some sorts?"

I grinned. "Nope. I think it means I just joined the choir." I sat down at the table, holding the slip of paper in my hand. *It's too fast.* I fought for breath. Michael sat down and tapped the paper. *Courage.*

He didn't say anything. When I shook my head, he tapped it again. "Take the leap, Linda. Or let the spirit wash over you or whatever that is."

I shrugged. "That just sounds weird."

"Then, think of it as a gift from Brendan. He's giving you something. You can't waste it."

I nodded. "Now, that seems a bit more normal." I stood up and reached for the paper. "It is a gift. A gift from Brendan." I put the paper in my pocket so it didn't get lost. "I guess I'm in the choir."

Later that night, I slipped into bed, moving Schnitzel sleeping by my pillow. I looked over at Michael and inhaled deeply. "Okay," I said.

"Okay to what?" he asked.

"I think I'm ready to see a medium."

"Yes." He punched his hand high in the air in victory. He leaned over his nightstand, opening the drawer. He waved the piece of paper in his hand with a flourish, his smile smug. "I just happen to have a list right here."

I laughed. "You've been waiting for this, haven't you?"

He shrugged. "I knew you'd come around. The spirit washing over you and all that."

"We're going to have to stop saying that."

He ran his finger down the list. "Rhonda has a waiting list that's over eight months."

"You called her?"

He shrugged. "I wanted to be ready. Just in case. Maybe we should check out the other names on the list."

I took the list and leaned back into my pillows. "Well, that is a long time." I scanned the names and pointed to one. "Her. I've read her book. She didn't sound too crazy."

I'd started reading books on mediums the first time Michael had mentioned one. It was research, one that required me to buy at least five or six books. I wanted to be ready, too.

Michael laughed. "Of course you've read her book."

He called the next day, but her waiting list was two years long. They offered him someone else, someone we could see in just a few weeks. He made the appointment.

Fantasia

Fantasia is a song that lets go of structure and rules. It spins an idea in many different ways. It's loose and airy and feels like an improvisation, as if the music is created from splashes of color and imagination. It becomes a fantasy, wrapping all around me, sparked by the divine.

It feels like magic.

34

Like most parents, when Michael and I had kids, we divided up our responsibilities. I cooked dinners while Michael did the food shopping. I helped with homework while he dragged out the garbage or took the cars in for an oil change. The same thing happened with our grief. I was the one who researched books and wrote thank you notes and hugged Zack or Lizzie when sorrow made them bicker and fight. Michael dealt with the logistics, like talking with the funeral director and the minister and even the neighbors. He also handled the police.

I couldn't talk with them, not even the detective with kind eyes, the one who promised me he'd uncover what really happened, the one who believed it was all an accident. I couldn't remember his name or even stay in the same room when Michael talked with him; my muscles trembled and I staggered away. So I froze that day in October when I saw his car pull into our driveway.

He wanted to update us. Michael had stayed home to meet with him. Snowy and Schnitzel scratched at the door, eager to greet him. I was upstairs, my hands gripping the stair banister. Michael looked up at me.

"I got this," he said and calmly slipped out the front door. I backed away, hidden in the hallway as I peeked through the window.

On Brendan's last day, I never saw the police and fire trucks in my driveway. I didn't hear the sirens blare through the neighborhood or see the flashing lights. But that's all I saw and heard when the detective opened his car door and walked toward our house. Michael shook his hand and they sat down on the front steps.

Bruce, Eileen's husband, had arranged for Michael to meet with the medical examiner the week before. He was willing to issue a new death certificate, one that didn't list suicide as the cause of death, but first, he needed the police's final report. We were waiting for that final report.

I backed away from the window and walked into Brendan's room, standing in front of his closet. His bed was gone, and Lizzie had wanted his metal desk, so I'd turned it into a vanity for her, with flower stickers winding around the sides. The day before, I'd taken out the shelving in his closet. I held my breath as I rummaged around his room, not sure what I might find. There was a stash of fruit snack wrappers on the floor. Underneath his sweatpants was an empty pizza box and a two-liter bottle of soda. I smiled but still worried with each new thing I found, terrified I was going to unearth something that made us realize the police had been right the first time.

My hand brushed against scraps of paper on the floor, hidden under his clothes. My fingers shook. *Are these notes?* Brendan never liked to talk about his feelings, but maybe he'd written about them.

When he was a toddler, our dog Peanut died suddenly. Brendan was sad but never talked about it. He started sleeping in the hallway. He never came into our room. In the morning, we'd find him huddled near the stairs, near us, but never bothering us. I hated knowing he was in pain and hid it from us.

I didn't want to find out he'd been in pain. That he'd hurt and hid it from me the same way he did when he was only three. I opened each scrap. One was a receipt for pizza he must have ordered when he was alone in the house. Another was an old math assignment. The last paper listed his screen names for his computer games. They all had to do with food. *I love steak. Taco King. Beefsteak.*

I put the list in the box on the card table in the middle of the room. I had two boxes on the table. One held memories, the parts of his life that made me smile, like his obsession with food. The other box was smaller, and held things I never thought I'd keep, but couldn't throw away. Sympathy cards. The bulletin for his service at the church. The book his friends and teachers signed at his funeral.

I picked up a stack of papers. His Bob stories. Every Sunday in third grade, he walked down the steps into the basement and typed up a story. Every single one started with, *One day a guy named Bob.* I placed them in the memory box.

I walked back into the hallway, peering over the wall and through the front door window. Michael and the detective were still talking. *Is he telling him it was an accident? Did they find new evidence?*

I walked back into Brendan's room, counting the steps. One, two, three . . . sixteen steps until I reached the table. I closed my eyes and took sixteen breaths and went back to sorting the items on the table. A sea urchin made out of soft rubber, with stretchy tentacles that attracted every speck of dust. Gooey toys, Brendan had called them. Even at fifteen, he loved fiddling with them. I put the toy in the memory box, trying to be grateful he had such a large box filled with fifteen years of memories.

I picked up the sympathy card from Brendan's CCD teacher. I placed it in the smaller box and then walked the sixteen steps into the hallway. They were still talking.

Sixteen steps back.

I picked up a note from Eddie, Brendan's best friend when he was in the fourth grade. My chest ached, but it made me remember years ago, when Brendan had rushed into the house after school and could barely make it into the bathroom. After the third day of the same thing, I was concerned and asked him what was going on.

"Nothing," he said, smirking. "Eddie and I made a bet. Every morning, I have to drink a giant bottle of water and then I can't go to the bathroom all day. I earn a dollar a day. So far I have seven dollars!"

I put the card into the bigger box. I walked the sixteen steps back and forth, each time placing something into one of the boxes until I came across a piece of paper I wasn't sure where it belonged. It was the last thing Brendan ever wrote, part of a summer project for school. He needed to make a video on a book he'd read about teen- agers living in a police state. I read it to help him and we sat in the den the day before he died, talking about the book. He wrote down a list of images for the video. *Burning books. Police state. Experiments on kids.* We left the paper on the kitchen counter so we could add to it. Michael texted with song ideas like "Revolution" and "Eve of Destruction."

The police would later read this paper, frowning with suspicion. They took pictures of it, as proof Brendan was a dark, depressed teenager.

I grabbed the paper, ready to throw it out. But the two of us had laughed as we worked on the project together. He listened to me, something a fifteen-year-old boy doesn't always do. He was grateful for my ideas and wrote some of them down. I'd seen hints of the adult he was becoming. I couldn't throw it away.

"He's gone," Michael called out. I ran down the stairs to the landing.

"What did he say?"

"He believes it was an accident."

I blew out my breath. "Thank God. Finally, he believes us."

"He believed us after the first day, after they found out about the challenge. But he wanted to make sure. He even interviewed Brendan's teachers and friends again. He's going to let the ME know, and then they'll issue a revised death certificate."

We'd been fighting for that for weeks. My stomach felt hollow inside. It was an empty victory. "What took so long? What were you talking about?"

Michael shrugged. "We were just talking. He's actually really nice. He told me about his best friend in high school. He died doing Whip-Its."

I sighed. Another stupid story of a teen pushing his limits, trying to get high by inhaling a cartridge of nitrous oxide. "And the note?" I asked, referring to the one I'd just placed in the memory box.

Michael shook his head. "He didn't think it was anything. Just something from a video game. He's closed the case. He ruled it an accident." He held up something in his hand. "He brought back his glasses."

I climbed down the next few steps, but then my knees weakened, and I sank to the landing. *His glasses. I can't believe I forgot about them.* The police had already returned his computer and his phone, but for some reason, they'd held onto his glasses.

Michael handed them to me. The silver frame was warm from the October sun. I held them in my hand, pretending for a moment, just a moment, it was Brendan's warmth.

I looked up at Michael. "I took him to a burger place when he learned he needed to wear glasses. He was so upset. He didn't want people looking at him. But the burger made him forget."

"Meat usually did."

I smiled and then held his glasses up to the light. "They're still dirty. He always kept them so dirty," I whispered. "And they always slid down his nose."

Michael laughed. "Remember when I thought he was getting some kind of tic because he kept jerking his head back? I thought there was something wrong with him, but he was just too lazy to push his glasses back up his nose."

I took off my own glasses and put his on, as if I could see through his eyes and look at the world the way he did. Everything blurred; his prescription was too strong for me. Still, I kept them on.

"Lights out. Glasses off. Head down," Michael said.

I took off his glasses and climbed the stairs. I counted the sixteen steps to the table. I placed his glasses in his box of memories, nestled between his Bob stories and a letter a girl wrote me last week, telling me Brendan had the most beautiful eyes she'd ever seen.

35

"It's a C," Argaille said to me as she hammered the note on the piano. I was at choir rehearsal, sitting in the soprano pew between Cheri and Laura. Including me, there were only four sopranos. Dianne sat next to the piano. I wanted to sit there, so I could hold onto the wood and feel the note vibrate beneath my fingers. But that was her spot, even though sometimes it was too loud for her. She put her head in her hands and winced. "Argaille, please. Can you just stop banging on the piano?"

It was my fault. Argaille was trying to give me my note. She pounded on the C, hoping I'd finally match the pitch. I could barely hear it. I was only ten feet away, but the note was a faint echo, unable to pierce through my fog of fear.

Dina, the alto who sat behind me, leaned forward. Her voice was made for church, with a vibrato that seemed to tremble with a message from God. Most times I tried to block out her notes because they were too close to mine, and I'd slide off my own and sing hers instead.

She sang my note for me. I nodded. I grabbed my pencil and circled the C in my music, but I knew it wouldn't help. Each time I pushed past the lump in my throat, my voice came out strangled, landing somewhere between a B and C. It didn't even stay there but wobbled back and forth, a tormented vibrato that made me cringe.

I was stunned at my capacity to sing notes that didn't exist. As a pianist, I sang the notes while I played them. They became a part of me, but I couldn't seem to find them when someone else played them.

"That's a lovely choice, dear," Argaille said. "Very creative."

I couldn't help smiling as she gushed over my wrong note. She taught music to young children and was so gentle with her corrections. She put her hands over her heart. "It's so interesting, maybe we'll even change the music to reflect your creativity. But first, let's try it one more time with the right note. Let's see if we can make that work."

I took a deep breath. *I can do this.* I'd already done something much harder. I'd sung the hymns at Brendan's funeral. This was only one note.

But I couldn't do it. Tears blurred my eyes. I'd already tried to quit the choir. The first time I sang with them during service, I went to Argaille and told her I couldn't do it. She nodded but then danced her hands in the air. She spoke about the Divine Flow and the Universe. Her choir robe swayed as she flapped her arms like the wings of a butterfly. I was lulled by her words and her robe blowing back and forth. She made it impossible for me to say no. I nodded and promised to return to rehearsal the next Thursday night.

I kept coming back. Some of it was Argaille and her strange way of arguing with me. Another reason was Brendan. He'd given me the song "Courage." It was a gift. I was afraid if I rejected it, he wouldn't give me any more signs. And then there was Bob, who sat behind me in choir and sang just like my father did.

I tried singing the C again and suddenly, Argaille stopped playing and clapped her hands. "I have an idea. Let's try a different warm-up. Everyone turn to the right and gently massage each other's shoulders."

I laughed at the groans from the pew behind me. Bob and Bruce. I thought of them as the Cranky B Boys because they grumbled whenever Argaille droned on too long or invented a new warm-up or made us sing a song they hated. Bruce was the bass and had a voice gentle and pure. He played the bagpipes, and that seemed so right because he looked just like a Scottish Santa.

"Come on, everyone. Turn to your right and start massaging!"

I turned to Laura, the soprano on my right. She had a soft smile and smelled like baby powder. I always stole her pencil accidentally, but she never seemed to mind. I rubbed circles on her shoulders. I could feel Cheri rubbing mine; she was shorter than me and probably on her toes, stretching to reach my shoulders.

Argaille clapped her hands. "Let's try it again," she said and turned back to the piano. My muscles were more relaxed now. This time, I didn't try to match the other sopranos. Instead, I listened to Bob and Bruce. They sang the bottom notes and I leaned on them, like a foundation holding me up. I didn't strain to reach for my notes. I landed on them softly, as if they'd been waiting for me. The written music was like a map, showing me where to go, but it was only when I ignored it and felt for my notes that I finally found my direction.

I sang and became one small part of the puzzle. I heard Dina's alto but stayed on my own notes. All four parts—soprano, alto, tenor and bass—clicked together and somehow added up to so much more than four.

"That's it!" Argaille yelled, her face tilted toward the ceiling. She stomped her feet as she continued to play. "That's it. Pray the song. Pray it!"

Her words pulled me out. Fear slammed into me, and once again, I lost my way. But I finally understood what Argaille meant when she talked about the Divine Flow. I'd had a little taste of it, could feel its power building inside me. I understood why she leaned back on her piano bench and shouted to the heavens. That feeling lasted less than a minute, but it was enough to keep me coming back to choir.

36

I was promised dreams. From the moment my son died, friends told me of dreams of parents and friends they'd lost. "He'll come to you," they said. "Just stay open." I clung to that hope each night, trying my best to believe, desperate to grab a glimpse of Brendan. Even my mother, who rarely spoke of my sister, told me that Elizabeth came to her in dreams. She'd never told me that before. I'd never dreamt of Elizabeth, only nightmares that kept me awake for hours.

I wanted to dream about Brendan, not these shadowy dreams that made no sense.

"You need to invite him in," my friends said.

I asked. I begged. I wrote notes to him. I ordered books on dreams. I kept a notepad by my bed so I could write down what I heard or saw. I woke each morning with nothing from Brendan. And yet, I could feel something. By the end of October, I finally knew what I was dreaming about. The harp.

I don't know why. I'd never wanted to learn the harp. I'd always planned on learning the cello, even more after Brendan died. I feared the darkness of the coming winter and needed a distraction. I researched teachers. But each time I took a step toward the cello, I'd dream about the harp. I woke with an ache that wouldn't leave me.

"Who plays the harp?" I asked my friends. "It seems so cliché."

I pushed away my dreams. I didn't write them down in the note-book by my bed. Instead, I filled out the rental form for a cello. I chose a teacher. The harp was too delicate, too ethereal. I wanted the heaviness of the cello. I wanted to scrape a bow across strings and feel the dark, mournful sounds press against my chest. I didn't want a celestial plucking that disappeared in seconds.

But my dreams never stopped. I fell asleep searching for Brendan, and each morning I woke, my hands aching as if I'd played the harp throughout the night.

My dreams were like smoke, a wispy fragment of a harp that melted in the air. I couldn't see its shape or size or the color of its wood. But I felt the strings tremble against my fingertips. The vibrations flowed through me. They wrapped around my heart. Even during the day, when my dreams faded away, my fingers tingled, a pulse humming inside me like a whisper only I could hear.

It filled me with that same yearning I'd felt so many years before, when I'd stood before my piano, still sleeping, reaching for the keys. Only this time, I was in the shadows, reaching for something I couldn't even see, something I wasn't even sure was there.

There were days when I believed in nothing and days when I believed in it all. I sang the hymns on Sundays, but I still refused to say the prayers. I listened to the sermons while borrowing from other religions. I prayed the rosary like I did as a teenager. Late at night, I'd make up my own prayers, my fingers rubbing each wooden bead. I'd wake in the morning, as I had years before, the rosary still wrapped around my hand.

At breakfast, I read about mindfulness and staying in the present. I walked through a trail of trees, focusing on the birds calling out to one another, the sun streaming through the leaves and the gravel slipping into my sneakers and biting my feet. In the afternoons, I researched books by mediums, sometimes smirking and throwing the books across the room and yet, ordering more until they no longer fit on one shelf. At night, I lit the candles I'd nestled within rocks, whispering a Jewish prayer I wasn't sure how to pronounce.

It was a shallow dive, one that barely broke the surface. I was skimming, afraid of drowning in deeper waters. I collected parts of God like a giant box of Lego blocks with no instructions on how to piece them together.

Can I fit together the sermon at church with the songs Brendan sent us? What about that feeling that flowed through me when the bird tapped on my door? Or when I dreamt of the harp? Can I hold onto that and my rosary beads? Will that fit with the rules of religion? I never spread them out and hunted for deeper meaning in them. What if it were just a jumble of mismatched pieces?

A woman stood up in church one day, her voice quivering as she shared her joy. Her neighbor's tree had fallen during a storm, but no one had been hurt. She offered her thanks to God. "He saved them. God is good."

God is good. Can I believe that and still believe in a God that chose to let my son die? And is that what faith is all about, believing in only the good?

I wasn't sure how to fit any of these pieces together. I was afraid if I followed step-by-step directions, I'd build something that had no meaning for me, and so I gathered bits from all different directions. I collected each block, admiring each one for its beauty. I kept them jumbled, a giant bucket of mystery, too afraid to fit them into a final picture.

Michael had no trouble piecing them together. He decided that if he wanted a greater connection to Brendan, he'd need to join the church. That meant being baptized. So the Rev came over for dinner to discuss it. Michael's mom was staying with us for the week due to a storm that had knocked out the power in her apartment on Long Island. All week, Fran had tried to make her son smile.

"Tell me about the bird," she'd say as she wrapped her hand around his arm. "And the songs. Again," she kept saying. "Again." She begged like a child, desperate to chase away the shadows in his eyes.

She didn't care that he meant to join the church; she only wanted her son to smile again. Still I was nervous when Rev. Rick rang the doorbell. Choosing a different religion seemed like a giant step.

Zack and Lizzie ran down the stairs at the sound of the doorbell. We all sat down at the kitchen table still turned the wrong way. Michael carved the turkey breast with cranberry sauce, and I passed around the mashed potatoes and green beans I'd bought earlier in the day. We had beer and wine, and pound cake and cookies, way too much food for the six of us, but then, this was my first time entertaining someone in a long time, let alone a minister.

"It was sure nice hearing you sing up there with the choir," Rev. Rick said. "They're a small group, so every bit helps."

"She sounded beautiful," Fran said. "The best one in the group."

I smiled at her, shaking my head. "Not even close." My legs still shook when I sang. Just thinking about it made my stomach hurt. I reached for some pound cake and pretended to eat.

Once dessert was over, Zack and Lizzie got bored and drifted away. Rev. Rick leaned back in his chair and clapped his hands. "All right, let's get down to business. Let me tell you how joining the church works. It's a simple ceremony where we ask members to welcome you. Another family is joining as well, so you'd be with them."

"Doesn't he need to get baptized?" I asked.

Fran jumped up and reached over for our plates, piling them into the sink.

"Mom, I'll do that later. Sit down," Michael said. "We have a dishwasher."

She shook her head. "It'll only take a few minutes. I'm faster than a dishwasher. And better."

Rev. Rick took a sip of his beer. "I almost forgot that you need to get baptized. Yes. First we'll baptize him. We'll keep it simple. A little sprinkle of water and that's that."

I glanced over at Fran to see her reaction. She scrubbed the roasting pan, not seeming to notice the conversation.

"Now, I do have a few questions for you," Rev. Rick said. "Can you tell me why you want to become a Presbyterian?"

Michael drained the wine in his cup before answering. He was nervous about this part. He'd had a bar mitzvah, but not because he'd studied Hebrew or went to temple. A few months before he turned thirteen, he crammed with a tutor and learned to say the words phonetically, not understanding any of the meaning behind the ceremony.

"I didn't have a lot of religion growing up," he said slowly. "I didn't even know Jews and Christians shared part of the Bible. The first time you spoke about Moses, I was shocked. I didn't know you guys had him too." He looked down, his fingers crumbling a piece of pound cake. "I don't know the rules or even what I'm supposed to believe. But I want to feel Brendan more."

He looked up, his eyes shining with tears. "Brendan is with God.

I want to feel closer to God so I can be closer to Brendan. I just want to feel him more."

This was Michael. He didn't see the need to spend months studying. He didn't care that he had no real knowledge. He didn't stare at each puzzle piece like I did, trying to find the perfect picture. Or scan a list of dogma as if it were a legal contract. He wanted to feel Brendan. That's all that mattered to him.

I watched Rev. Rick's face, wondering if that would be enough or if there was some kind of checklist Michael would need to complete. But after a moment, Rev. Rick shrugged and reached for another cookie. "That's good enough for me. We welcome everyone, no matter where they are on their faith journey."

Michael smiled and ate a piece of his cake. The conversation turned to talk of sports, and I sat there, lost in my thoughts, wondering if it could ever be that simple for me. Suddenly, his mom jerked at the sink. She slammed the water off and whirled around, hands on her hips.

"Wait. What's this I'm hearing?"

I held my breath. This was the explosion I'd feared.

She yanked her chair out and sat down with a huff. "What are you talking about?" she asked, her voice hard.

"Baseball," Michael said slowly.

She nodded. "I thought so. I heard you talking about the Mets." She reached for her wine, her rings tapping against the glass. "I can't believe you're talking about the Mets." She shook her head. "What? Are you thinking about becoming a Met fan?" she demanded to know.

Michael leaned over and patted her hand. "No. Don't worry, Mom. I'm forever a Yankee fan."

She blew out her breath and poured herself some more wine,

shaking her head. "You had me worried there for a moment. I couldn't believe my ears. I mean, the Mets?"

I started laughing. "I'm sitting here worried you're going to be upset about Michael becoming a Presbyterian. That he's converting and turning his back on his heritage, his childhood faith. But you're more upset that he might become a Mets fan?"

She leaned back and smiled, a real one not like the polite ones she'd offered all night. Michael and Rev. Rick joined in my laughter. She took another deep sip of her wine before shrugging.

"What can I say?" she asked, her grin widening. "I really love the Yankees."

37

It was the morning of our appointment with the medium. The only thing that I knew was that his name was Joe and that he gave sessions out of a church for spiritualists. I wasn't sure what that meant, only that they believed they could speak to the dead.

I treated our visit like an experiment. I armed myself with hidden talismans, little tests I hoped Brendan would talk about during the reading. Inside my pocket was one of the wooden birds from my tote bag. My other pocket held bits of leaves and twigs I'd torn off bushes on my walk with the dogs. I wore an angel necklace but tucked it under my shirt.

I wanted proof. I didn't want vague assurances like, *You're wearing something that reminds you of your son.* I wanted specifics, like *There's a wooden bird in your pocket.*

The church was a small, white building with only a few windows. It looked more like a day care than a church. Inside was a small room with wooden pews and a stained-glass window. Statues of angels were scattered around the room.

Joe was waiting for us in the hallway. We'd raced into the church late because our car battery had died. Joe waved away our apologies and shook our hands. He looked like an Irish-Catholic priest with his silver hair, dark turtleneck, and round red cheeks.

"Welcome," he said and even his voice boomed like my childhood priest, the one who laughed whenever wiggling toddlers escaped their mother's arms and wandered up the aisle.

We walked into a tiny room that looked like a monk's cell, with a single bed, three chairs, and a small desk. He waved at us to sit down. We squirmed in our chairs, listening as Joe talked about his life as a seminarian, studying to become a Catholic priest. "I left the church once I realized my gift," he said. "Once I realized I could speak to the dead."

He seemed so sincere, so genuine. Exactly the kind of person who made people believe.

"Watch my body," he said. "Sometimes, I don't have the words. My body tells you more than I can say."

I almost rolled my eyes at that. It seemed like a way to explain away anything he got wrong. He spoke about surrounding himself in white light and started a prayer, the Our Father. I was surprised at something so conventional. I'd expected an invocation of spirits or a ritual lighting of a candle.

I grabbed Michael's hand when Joe closed his eyes and rocked back and forth. He said nothing. The only sound in the room was him rocking in the chair. We held our breath waiting. Finally, he spoke, his eyes still closed.

"Two men are coming forward. One is very tall, the other one shorter. The tall man is in the military. He's wearing a uniform. Wait. They're carrying someone. Another male." Joe opened his eyes. "That's my symbol for someone who recently passed. Does that make sense to you?"

We nodded. It wasn't enough, of course. I squeezed Michael's hand in warning. *Say nothing.* We'd told Joe nothing of why we were here. I didn't want him using any clues to convince us he was really talking to Brendan.

"I can't hear those who recently passed as well. The other men will speak for him." Joe frowned. "But this male is resisting. He doesn't want to be carried." He chuckled. "He's very independent. Wants to speak for himself. He's strong. He won't let them help. And I can almost hear him. Oh, he's strong. So very strong."

Michael and I leaned forward. I'd read in my books that mediums rarely offer specific details. Their words sketch a simple drawing and it's the listeners who fill in the outlines with their own images. He'd offered us nothing. Only a male that recently passed. But longing flowed inside me until I could almost convince myself I saw a faint picture of Brendan.

Joe groaned, his eyes still closed. "I can't hear what he's saying." He leaned back in his chair and we waited in the silence, our frustration growing. I wanted to run out of this strange place, but my legs were heavy and cold, frozen to the chair. I stayed for that tiny chance that Brendan might give us a message.

"There's an older woman here. She feels like a grandmother. I'm going to move to her."

There was another long stretch of silence. They didn't show this on TV, these long depressing pauses that made you doubt everything. Joe's chair rattled, a metallic ping as his arm moved back and forth. I pressed my leg against Michael's and jerked my chin toward Joe.

"Look at his arm," I whispered. *Watch my body,* Joe had said. His arm shook against the chair, his fingers curled into a ball just like my grandmother who had Parkinson's disease.

"I'm feeling love," he said with a sigh. "But I can't hear what she's saying." He shook his head. "There's a young woman here. I'm going to talk to her."

Another round of silence and once again, I filled in his outline with my own desire. *My sister?*

Joe rubbed his forehead. "She's young. A child."

I said nothing. His hands, no longer shaking, cradled his head. "I have a headache," he said, moaning. "I can't seem to concentrate."

I no longer saw Joe, but my sister shaking in her bed the morning before she'd died. Her groans had pulled me from sleep, the tumors invading her brain. "It's too much," Joe said. "I need to move on. Is that okay?"

"Of course," Michael said.

The spell broken, I looked at the clock on the desk. Twenty minutes had passed. So far we had nothing except for a shaking hand and a headache. He'd given us the barest outline; I was the one who filled in grandmother and sister. Not Joe. I took a deep breath. I wanted facts. Not feelings.

"The male is back." Joe smiled. "He's still not letting others speak for him. But I can feel him better now. He's funny. Smart. Very smart. He tells jokes; the kind that not everyone gets. He's witty. And likes puzzles. He's quite the thinker."

He cleared his throat. He still hadn't offered any proof, but he was describing Brendan. "He thinks differently. Outside of the box. Oh, he makes me laugh." He chuckled.

I want the bird, Brendan. Tell him I have a bird in my pocket.

Joe coughed. "Excuse me." He took a sip of water from the bottle on his desk. "This male is sarcastic." His voice roughened, as if his words splintered inside him. "He's always around you. Sending you signs. He's showing me the months of June and September."

Michael and I looked at each other. Those months were Lizzie's and Zack's birthdays. Michael's hand tightened around mine. I wanted more.

Joe coughed into his hand and then touched his throat. "He's younger than I thought. But he feels old. So much older than his years." His fingers pulled back on his collar, stretching his turtleneck. "Why, he's just a teenager."

He twisted his head back and forth and cleared his throat. "He's a boy. Just a boy." Tears slid down his cheeks. He cleared his throat, both hands now rubbing his neck.

"I can't seem to breathe," he whispered. His chest heaved up and down. We stared at him. He'd told us to watch his body. I shook my head, trying to erase the image I had never wanted to see.

Is this . . . is this Brendan's last moments?

Michael turned to me, but I couldn't look at his anguish. I stared straight ahead at Joe, watching him squirm in his chair, fighting for air.

"I can't breathe," he said.

Michael crushed my hand. Joe's breath burst out of him, raw gasps that pierced my heart. "He didn't know," Joe said between pants. "He never would have—Oh, he didn't know."

Please.

Stop.

We said nothing, only sat there, clinging to each other, helpless as we listened to Joe struggle for breath. After a few minutes, his gasps slowed and his hands fell into his lap. He drew in a ragged breath. "I felt as if I couldn't breathe." He opened his eyes. "Does any of this make sense to you?"

I said nothing at first. When Michael had booked the appointment, he'd told him our last name. Before we came, I'd googled Brendan online to see what the medium might learn about him. I found nothing about the way he'd died. He was listed in the newspaper as an honors student. There were articles about his track team. His obituary mentioned his love of food. This was what I'd expected to hear. I'd wanted to leave with a picture of my son as a smart teenager who loved to feel the wind against him as he rode his bike. I didn't expect to watch a horror movie of his last moments.

Joe stared at us and finally, I nodded.

"It's our son."

After a while, Joe's breathing slowed. He leaned forward and grabbed both of our hands. "I feel his love. He's sending love. So much love." He shuddered and bowed his head. I stared down at our hands, the three of us tangled together. Joe's hands were thick and covered in calluses, but I didn't feel them. At that moment, it wasn't Joe's hand holding mine. It was Brendan's hand.

His long fingers like mine. The hand I'd held when we skipped down the block to the kindergarten bus. The hand I molded over an apple at our first piano lesson. The hand he sometimes let me hold late at night when we watched shows together after everyone else had gone to bed.

Love flowed from one hand to another. I could almost see it. It moved like water, weaving into the cracks inside me. It curled around my heart, washing away the memory of Joe fighting for air. It was a feeling. Just a feeling, nothing I could prove, nothing I could hold onto late at night, but oh, it felt so good.

Michael nudged my leg with his knee. *He's here.*

I closed my eyes and let myself feel.

Yes.

"He's so sorry," Joe whispered, his head still bowed. "I can hear him so clearly now. He's telling me he's sorry. So very sorry. He didn't know."

I couldn't help smiling. It's what Brendan said each time he did something wrong. "I didn't know," he said when he broke his arm jumping off the couch. "I didn't know," he said when he shattered my vase. "I didn't know." And of course, I always forgave him.

Joe looked up at us. "He wants to know if you're going to be all right."

I almost laughed. *Will I ever be all right?*

But, even as I wanted to say no, I knew the answer. We would be all right. I could feel the love flowing through me. I almost wanted to push it away, as if I had no right to feel this sense of peace inside me. But it felt so good. The hands around mine squeezed tighter and I held on.

"We'll be okay," Michael said. "Tell him not to worry. We'll be okay."

"He didn't know," Joe said again. "He's so sorry."

Something loosened inside me. I'd been filled with rage at the doctors, the detective, the people who'd spread rumors. I'd learned to let that go. But deep within, there was a secret part of me still angry at Brendan. I don't even think I realized it was a low hum inside me, a refrain that forever played. *How could he have done something so stupid?*

Joe kept saying he was sorry, and I did what the books on mediums warned me not to do. I heard only Brendan. It wasn't Joe, but my child begging for forgiveness.

I'm so sorry. I didn't know.

My anger slipped away.

I came here hoping to hear about the wooden bird in my pocket. A small scrap of hope that Brendan was around me. I didn't expect to be overwhelmed by the love flowing between us. I didn't expect to offer my son forgiveness and feel the cold knot of anger inside me dissolve.

I didn't know.

It was a whisper inside me. I answered back. *I forgive you.*

Peace crept inside me. I held on to it, wrapping it around me like a blanket. "It's okay, Brendan," I said out loud, squeezing the tangle of our hands. "We're going to be okay."

And for the first time, I believed it. We were going to be okay.

38

We hadn't told the kids about Joe before we went. We'd planned on telling them over the weekend, but as soon as they walked through the door that afternoon, we pounced on them. We didn't tell them about the long pauses or when Joe's voice clenched. We focused on the message of love and Brendan calling out June and September. Lizzie cried tears of joy, her lower lip quivering as she smiled. Zack punched his fist high above him in victory.

Their excitement fed mine. I ran upstairs into my room and closed the door. I called Hedy and Eileen. Then Trudy and Patty and Becky. I called everyone. With each retelling, I honed my story, glossing over any moments of confusion, those pauses filled with nothing. By the time I called my cousin Nancy, I knew just how to say the story, where to pause for dramatic effect and when to lower my voice to a whisper.

"I'm so happy for you guys," Nancy said, and I hung up the phone, smiling. I wrote down each thing Joe said, each proof that I could point to and say, *See? My son is always around me.* I looked at the list, my pencil tapping against the paper, moving faster and faster. There was something growing inside me, a frustration that made my fingers shake. Joe had given us messages of love. Confirmation that this was an accident. He gave us peace. That should have been enough. But it wasn't. Brendan had more to say.

I tossed the notebook away. I flung open my bedroom door and ran downstairs. Michael was sitting in the den, my laptop open in front of him. He looked up. "Finished telling everyone?"

"There's something more." My words came out of me in one breath. I shook my head and tried again. "He needs to tell us something. There's more. I know this is going to sound crazy, but—"

Michael held up his hand. "I know. We need to go to another medium."

Hearing it out loud should have stopped me. It should have sounded crazy to already be talking about going to another medium. But it didn't. "You feel it too?"

He nodded. "He wants to tell us something else." He pointed to the laptop. "I found one. It's one you bookmarked."

I squinted at the screen. I didn't remember bookmarking a medium, but, then, I had a pile of books on my dresser that I didn't remember ordering. I must have done it late one night.

Michael smiled. "He's in the city. On the Upper West Side. I already called him. His name is Glenn."

I waited. "And?"

"We have an appointment Wednesday."

As a child, I believed the sacred could be found only in church. I loved lighting candles there, slipping my money into the slot, reaching for the long wooden stick and staring at a flickering light. When we lit candles at home, though, they were merely a decoration, as if God existed only through the church or a priest. But after Joe, I started seeing birds as not just a message of hope, but as something sacred. It seemed as if everywhere I looked, there was a message for me. I walked among trees, holding my breath as sunlight struck a dewdrop resting on a leaf. I bent over the mums on my front steps, watching a bee crawl around petals. And when we drove into the city to see the second medium, I looked at the line of trucks and cars waiting to go through the Lincoln Tunnel, as if they too, were sending me a sacred message.

We didn't tell anyone about this visit. Another medium? Within a week of the first one? It seemed a bit crazy. Glenn lived on the Upper West Side, in an apartment so forgettable nothing stood out except for The Beatles poster hanging on his wall. He looked like an ex-Beatle, with his bowl haircut, blue jeans, and boyish smile. We'd blocked our phone number when we called, telling him nothing but our first names. Michael had stuffed a wad of cash into his pocket so we didn't have to use our credit card. I imagined a receptionist who scanned our card and then researched us while we sat in the waiting room. But it was just him. He didn't ask for money at the beginning of the session or even our last name.

He said a prayer before we started, just like Joe. He spoke of the same white light and then drifted off into a trance. After a minute, he snapped his eyes open and began to speak. He didn't pause or search for his words; they spilled out of him like water.

After the session, I made a chart of his comments. I divided it into two categories. The first were vague guesses anyone could make, like when he looked down at our hands clasped together. "He's saying he loves you guys so much." Or when he told us my dad wasn't a believer. "He's a skepticist, Brendan is saying." Glenn laughed. "And he's saying skepticist is too a word. Look it up in the dictionary."

Later, I found the word in the dictionary, but still placed his comment in the good guess column. The second column was for things

Glenn couldn't have known. They were my bullet points of proof, like when Glenn pointed at Michael. "He wants you to have the party. He wants you to celebrate your love. And he'll be dancing with you."

Michael's eyes had widened. Later, he told me he'd been thinking about having a party for our twenty-fifth anniversary in a few years, but doubted he could celebrate anything. *I can't have a party*, he thought on the ride into the city. But now, Brendan was telling him to have the party.

Then Glenn turned to me, his eyes crinkled. I held my breath. At that moment, he almost looked like Brendan. Glenn smiled at me and reached across the table to pat my hand. "He wants you to know that he stands behind you when you write. He wraps his arms around you and whispers words."

The week before Joe had reached out and held our hands. I'd felt Brendan's love flow from hand to hand. I'd thought that would be enough. But oh, Glenn had just given me an image that I'd hold forever in my heart. I wrote each morning and loved imagining Brendan writing with me.

"He's helping you write," Glenn said. "He wants you to remember that inspiration means 'in spirit.'" My hand flew to my mouth. Those were the exact words I'd written in my journal the day before.

I wrote that down in the second column, proofs I could point to when I began to doubt. One bullet point might not be enough for me, but stacked together, they had power.

My favorite point was when Glenn cocked his head and listened within. "I feel such a connection to this kid. He's funny. And sarcastic. I like that." He paused and then laughed, a private joke he never shared. And then he jerked and held up a finger.

"Wait, he's telling me we have an even greater connection." He squeezed his eyes shut and then snapped them open with a laugh.

"Well, that's it. That's why I feel him so strongly. Turns out we share the same birthday."

We'd told him nothing about Brendan. Nothing about ourselves. There was no way he could have known that. He reached behind him and pulled out his wallet. I almost told him he didn't need to show us, but I'm so glad he did. He tugged his driver's license out and handed it to me. I smiled. July 12th.

When I told friends the stories of the mediums, I saved that one for last. It made everyone but my dad believe.

At the end of the session, Glenn clapped his hands together and stood up. He held out his hand, waiting for us to stand and say good-bye. Before we could shake his hand, though, he froze. "Wait, he's giving me one last image." He chuckled. "Oh, this kid is quite the character. He's turned into Harry Potter."

Michael and I smiled. Brendan hated whenever his aunts and uncles told him he looked like Harry Potter. Everyone thought he looked like him, but we had never seen it. When our whole family went to the Harry Potter ride at Universal, my brother Allan was convinced we'd be ushered to the front of the line once they saw Brendan.

"He's wearing a big black cape." Glenn said. "And a top hat. He's waving a magic wand all around you, throwing sparks of love. He's saying goodbye. He wants you to believe." Glenn reached around us, his hands waving in the air. He curled his fingers as if he were grabbing invisible sparks.

He stared down at his open palms. "It's so colorful," he said and his voice was filled with awe. He moved his hands back and forth, holding a ball of color and light. I saw nothing. I looked at Michael and he shook his head. Still, we twisted in our seats, straining toward those invisible sparks. I wanted to put my hand out and catch them like fireflies in the night.

"It's beautiful," Glenn said and Michael and I both sighed as if we could feel them. Glenn pressed his hands to his heart. "I'm going to remember this. It's a gift," he said. "A beautiful gift."

I had a long list of bullet points. The birthday. The word *inspiration*. And when Glenn told us he saw Michael's father building a sandwich, slowly layering on each slice of meat with meticulous care. That was Ben. There was even a glass of his favorite drink—celery soda. Most people didn't even know that was a real drink. I stared at my list at night.

In college, I used to do algebraic problems before going to bed. I loved working on the equations, writing each proof down until the final one pinged inside me, saying, *Yes, this is proven*. There was no doubt; the math made everyone believe. I did that at night, with my two columns, hunting for proof to ping inside me, staring at all the things that made me believe.

But it was the feeling that seduced me. Somehow, those sparks of love swirled around me, floating in the air. They were like little stars of light. I couldn't see them. They didn't belong in the equation.

I didn't care because I could feel them. After Michael fell asleep, I closed my eyes and played with the sparks. I imagined their colors dancing all around me, landing on my shoulders, my arm. My heart. They didn't burn or disappear in a wisp of smoke. They seeped inside, flowing around me, filling me.

It was just a feeling, nothing more. But I believed.

39

As the mother of three children, I'd experimented with different ways to limit sibling rivalry. I made sure to give an equal number of Christmas presents. Each child had their own day during the week, a day where they were allowed to choose where to sit and to pick their favorite dinner. I tried to make each one feel special, to honor each one's unique strengths.

But like most kids, they still complained and questioned why they didn't get the yellow cup or the bigger half of a cookie. Even after Brendan died, they still found a way to be jealous. In the fall, I had cut down a wooden pallet. I stained it and then mounted pictures of all three kids. We'd recently painted the den and the walls were empty. I needed our whole family in the room. Zack and Lizzie stood before it, scanning the pictures, their fingers counting in the air.

"How come Brendan is in more pictures?" Zack asked.

"Yeah," Lizzie said. "I'm in four, but Brendan is in six!"

They weren't just jealous of the pictures. One night, after I picked up Lizzie from dance class, and when she didn't run into the car chattering about turns and pliés, I knew something was wrong. It was early December and cold. Her breath came out like white smoke, even in the car. She shook her head when I asked and said nothing on the ride home. She stomped into the house.

"I want my own sign." She dragged out the word sign until it became a whine.

I wrapped my arm around her shoulder. "He's given us so much. The birds. The songs."

She twisted away. "They're all Daddy's signs. And yours. I want my own." Her lips pushed into a pout. "I want my own, from Bre-Bre."

Brendan had hated that nickname, except from Lizzie. Sometimes, Zack tortured him with that name, his lips forming the words without making a sound, throwing his brother into an angry frenzy.

"Make him stop," Brendan yelled.

"What?" Zack asked innocently, his arms held out wide. "I'm only blowing him kisses."

Lizzie was the only one who could use that nickname. I smiled, picturing the way Brendan would melt whenever she called him that.

"Don't laugh at me." Lizzie yanked her dance bag off her shoulder and threw it onto the floor. Schnitzel and Snowy came running over, their tails wagging, but she didn't even stop to pet them.

"Sweetie, I'm not laughing. I'm trying to help you."

She stood there, her hands fisted, her shoulders so tight they touched her ears. I wanted to hold her, to stop her from trembling, but she looked as if she'd shatter if I touched her. I reached down and picked up her bag, not sure what I should do. I wished Michael were here, but he was still driving home from work. *He'd tell a joke right now.* Something that made her smile and forget the pain and anger running through her. I picked at the stitching on her bag, trying to remember something funny, anything, even a knock-knock joke.

I worked a loop out of the stitching and I pulled it, snapping the thread. I'd learned to live with the pain inside of me, to move around the broken shards and survive. But this was different. This was my daughter, trembling with pain over losing her brother. It broke my heart. We could walk outside together and cry under the stars, but she wanted something more. Her own connection, her own piece of Brendan, like the nickname only she could use.

I sat down on the front steps, knowing she needed something I couldn't give her. I scratched at the stitching and closed my eyes, wishing again that Michael were here. I didn't know how to help her. I took a few deep breaths until I heard footsteps.

"It's okay," Zack said. "Shh, it's okay." I looked up. Zack's hand was on Lizzie's shoulder. "It's not always going to be like this."

He seemed so grown-up. Zack had turned thirteen a month after Brendan died. I did everything to make it a normal day. We gave him presents and invited family over. He went to White Castle with Michael to binge on tiny hamburgers. We tried so hard to make it a celebration and still, that night, he turned to me, his hand on his chest. "Will it always be like this?"

His words cracked something inside me. I wanted to reach out and take away his pain, to lift the heaviness that pressed against him.

"I know this feels like the end of the world," I said. "It is. But we won't always feel like this because together we will make a new one, a world where Brendan is part of us in a different way."

A part of me hated that my sister's death had prepared me to comfort my own children. I knew exactly what they were feeling. I needed to acknowledge their pain. I'd spent the past few months telling stories and trying so hard to rebuild our new world. Most days it felt like I did nothing, but now, watching Zack comfort his sister, I knew my words had reached him.

Lizzie leaned into him and he wrapped one arm around her. "It's okay," he murmured. "I know what's going to make you feel better. Let's watch a show together."

I thought she'd push him away like she did me, but she nodded and allowed herself to be guided into the den. He pulled her down onto the couch. I followed, still holding her bag, my heart breaking for different reasons.

Zack and Lizzie were the siblings who bickered and played together. He was the brother she loved to do art projects with and run outside in the snow to catch snowflakes on their tongues. They planned sleepovers and printed out agendas for each hour of the night. Brendan was the big brother who cuddled her when she was sad. He was the one who invented his "Shoe Time" song. He sang and danced his song whenever she cried as a baby. He was the one who kissed her and tucked her hair behind her ears and wiped away her tears. He was the one who comforted her.

I clutched Lizzie's bag as I watched Zack take over Brendan's role.

They sat so close together on the couch. Zack reached around her and fumbled for the remote. He'd been watching something and had paused it when he'd heard his sister cry. "We're going to sit and watch TV together and you're going to feel all better."

He sounded so mature. So calm and reasoned. I sighed. He sounded like Brendan.

He un-paused the TV. It was a singing competition show, one we'd never watched before. It looked like a flashy gimmick, with the judges facing backward listening to a contestant, ready to push their buttons and spin around.

Perfect. She's going to love this show. I opened the closet door, ready to hang up the dance bag, but then froze when I recognized the song. I walked back into the den and sat down next to them.

"Listen," Zack whispered. "I paused it just in time. Listen to what song he's singing."

"Knockin' on Heaven's Door."

We'd heard the song many times since Michael had walked into the house and shared Brendan's song with us. Each time the opening chords sounded, we stopped talking and felt the magic wash over us. Zack put down his phone. Lizzie stopped playing with the dogs and Michael and I closed our eyes and held each other's hand, our family of five complete. I said yes each time I heard it.

But this. This felt like more than wonder. This was both of my sons finding a way to comfort their sister. It filled my heart as a mother, the same way it did when I'd watch the three of them play together. This was love.

Lizzie fumbled for my hand and I squeezed her fingers. "Brendan gave me a sign," she whispered. "My own sign." The three of us sat there, listening to the song. When it was over, we looked at each other and started laughing.

"I knew I could make you feel better," Zack said with a satisfied nod.

Lizzie leaned her head on his shoulder and together, they watched the rest of the show.

40

I dreamt about harps a few nights a week. In the morning, when the tingling in my fingers faded, I couldn't help wondering about fate. Was there something pushing me to play the harp? It wasn't just that. Why did I feel so compelled to join a church before Brendan died? Was his death fated? Did I know?

And why did I buy those birdhouses the week before he died?

I'd wandered the aisles of the craft store, searching for decorations for fall. I filled my basket with red and yellow silk leaves and orange pumpkins. There was no more room in my basket, but then I spotted a wooden birdhouse, shaped like a church with a steeple on top and two swinging doors. I'd seen the shelf of birdhouses before. I'd probably walked by it dozens of times in the past, but that day, it was irresistible. I squished down some leaves and placed the birdhouse in the cart. A minute later, I wheeled the cart around and put it back on the shelf.

I hate birds. I won't even let Michael hang a bird feeder on our tree. What am I going to do with a birdhouse?

But something inside me pushed me. Three times I returned to the shelf, each time putting a few more birdhouses into my cart until they nearly toppled over the sides. I came home with a giant bag filled with seven different birdhouses, each one wrapped in paper. Brendan watched me take each one out. I unwrapped the paper and placed them on the counter, waving at the village of birdhouses.

"What do you think?" I asked him.

He walked around the counter, inspecting each one. "What are they for?"

"For decoration. I'm going to paint them different colors and put them on the deck. It will really brighten it up."

"Did you get birdseed?"

I laughed. "Of course not. You know I don't want any birds near the house."

He poked at one of the doors, swinging it open. "Maybe they'll still come. Can birds fit inside?"

I hadn't thought of that. "Well, I'll probably glue the doors shut. Maybe dad knows of a chemical that keeps birds away."

He shook his head. "Who buys birdhouses when they're terrified of birds? And seven of them?" He walked away, still shaking his head, his arms out wide in a shrug.

There was another dream I started having, but this one was more like a daydream. It was such a strange thought, something that made no sense to me at all. *Brendan wants us to go to Seattle.*

I felt those words day after day, like a drumbeat pounding inside me. *Seattle. Go to Seattle.* After a week of feeling this message, I fell asleep during the day. I woke an hour later with a startled jerk. *Seattle is a port to Alaska. Brendan wants us to go on a cruise to Alaska.*

I pushed aside the thought, knowing it was madness, but then I walked to my mailbox. Inside was a brochure for cruises. I stared down at the page for an Alaskan cruise. *Is this fate?* I reached for my phone, my fingers fumbling as I texted Michael to tell him what had happened and that Brendan wanted us to go on a cruise. He would believe me. Of course he would. I couldn't seem to catch my breath as I waited. I saw the dot dot dot as he typed his response, but then it disappeared. A minute later it was back and then gone again. I put the phone down on the table and took a few deep breaths. I kept my eyes closed until I heard the phone buzz with his answer.

I can't.

I shook my head. He said no? Not Michael who believed in everything, who spread his arms wide and dove right into a feeling. Now I was the one ready to book a cruise that afternoon.

I can't go on a vacation, he texted. *Not without him. Not yet. Maybe next year.*

He believed in the message, but he couldn't go away, not when it would only be the four of us. He was too afraid of the pain. I understood that; I hated the number four. At church, I counted the number of people in each family. I burned with envy each time I saw a family of five. So I dropped it. I didn't bring it up again. I pushed away the drumbeat inside me until my own doubts washed away even the faintest trace of it.

41

Toward the end of January, we hosted a brunch for my family and the families of Brendan's best friends. Tim, Alex, and Tony gathered up cans of Mountain Dew and bags of chips and went downstairs into the basement with Zack and his cousins to play video games. If I closed my eyes, it seemed like the party we'd hosted over the summer, when the boys had disappeared, reappearing occasionally to load their plates full of chicken saté and clams with caramelized garlic.

I tried not to look at Brendan's friends too closely. At fifteen, they were changing quickly. I didn't want to know if they'd grown taller or if their faces had thinned out.

I made Brendan's favorite foods for the party. In the oven was a tray of ham and Swiss sliders baked with garlic butter. My mother made baked ziti with meatballs and sausage, and Lizzie had doubled her recipe for Reuben dip. Like most parties, this one divided into groups with my family sitting at the dining room table and the three families of Brendan's friends on the benches in the breakfast bar. I floated from family to friends, smiling at the stories of Brendan.

"I heard all about Brendan and his love of food before I even met him," Alex's dad told me. "I was amazed how he could eat so much."

Laura, Tim's mom, brought me pictures of the boys. I never sat down, never ate. The stories were enough to feed me.

"Any more signs?" Tony's dad, Matt, asked when I walked over with a plate full of calzones. He loved to hear about the signs. I told them about the songs and the medium and the two wooden birds I'd found in the house. I wasn't sure if all six sitting at the table believed, but Matt's enthusiasm was enough for me to tell story after story.

"Oh, my God," he said, his eyes round. He nudged his wife, Michele, with his elbow. "Are you hearing this? All these signs? Brendan is so strong."

I smiled. This was why I loved telling the stories. Not just because it helped to validate them, but because it was a chance to speak about Brendan in the present tense, to use the word is instead of was. *He is strong. He leaves me messages. He helps me.* He wasn't forever fifteen when I spoke about the signs.

"I asked the medium if the songs were real," I said. It was the only question I'd asked him. I didn't want to lead him, but I was desperate to know if the songs Michael kept bringing home were real signs. Michael had four playlists by now, but three songs meant the most to me.

The first song, "Knockin' on Heaven's Door," made me believe Brendan was with God. The second song, "Courage," pushed me to find my voice and sing with the choir. But the third song meant the most. It was from that day Michael had held out his hand asking me to feel Brendan. "Have a Little Faith in Me." I didn't at the time, but now I did. It was my reminder that even if I couldn't feel him, he was still near me. His love would light the way as long as I had faith in him.

We even had the words, "Have a Little Faith in Me," inscribed on his tombstone. I was afraid to ask Glenn about the songs that day, afraid he'd only tell me what I wanted to hear, but I was desperate to know if the songs were real.

Matt leaned forward. "What did the medium say?"

"He said the songs are real. Actually, he said, 'You know they are.'" I shrugged. "But that wasn't enough for me. I needed more. So I asked again."

Are the songs real?

I'd said nothing more that day, sitting in Glenn's apartment. Nothing about heaven or courage or faith. I just waited, my hand reaching for Michael's, while Glenn looked beyond us, hearing something I desperately wished I could hear.

For a moment, I got lost in that memory. Matt slammed his hand onto the table. "You're killing me, here. What did the medium say?"

I smiled. "At first, he just looked at me for a long time. And I figured, that's it. Just a few generic words that could mean anything. But then he winked at me. 'Have a little faith,' he said. 'Have a little faith.'"

"Oh my God. That's incredible," Matt said, and everyone nodded. Joy bubbled up within me.

"There's more," I said. I hadn't told anyone this story because it pushed the boundaries of belief. But the awe in Matt's face gave me courage. "Well, the first time we went to the medium, my car battery died. We didn't think anything of it. But a week or so before Christmas, it died again. We still didn't think anything of it."

"Ooh," Matt said, rubbing his hands. "This is going to be good."

"A neighbor gave me a jump and that was that. But, a few days later, the battery died again. Again, I really didn't think anything of it. We took it in to get a new battery." I paused, drawing out the suspense. "The next day . . . it dies again. Now, we're mad, thinking the mechanic scammed us. So we switch mechanics, and the new one installs another battery. The next day—"

"No way," Matt said. "It died again?"

I grinned. "Yep." By now, Michael had come up next to me, listening. He grinned and bounced on his toes in excitement, knowing what I was about to say.

"So a few days go by and everything seems fine. And then? Michael's car battery dies. So we get it replaced. Battery dies the next day. The mechanic checks everything. Couldn't figure out what was wrong. So, he replaced the battery again. The next day? Dies again." I paused, not sure if I should say the next part.

"But she hasn't even said the crazy part yet." Michael said. "My car dies again, and I'm getting ready to jumpstart it. But Linda says no, she has this feeling. A feeling. She walks outside, touches the car, and asks Brendan to turn it on."

He paused to make sure everyone was listening. "And it works."

Every face at the table looked at me with awe. "And get this," Michael continued. "A few days later, I was at the gas station, and the car dies. I'm waiting for the guy to give me a jump. I was afraid I'd miss my train, so I called Linda. She asked Brendan *over the phone*, and then, boom. The car worked."

I smiled at their gasps, but then I looked to my left and saw my brother Jim standing in the kitchen, halfway between my family and my friends. He stood with his legs hip-distance apart, his arms crossed behind his back. I'd seen him stand this way dozens of times. Brendan used to stand the same way, especially when he was deep in thought. But that day, I didn't see a reflective pose in my brother; I saw only skepticism.

In general, my family accepted the premise that Brendan was around us. *He's always in our hearts.* But when it came to specifics, like saying that the bird was a message from Brendan, well, that's when eyebrows were raised, or worse, condescending platitudes were offered that hid their doubts. *That must make you feel good.*

A few days before the party, my father had come over, carrying his metal tool box, the one where he kept all his electrical equipment. He wore his Daddy fix face. The backyard lights had been turning off while I was teaching piano. They'd turn on, but after a few hours, they'd switch off on their own. I didn't say it was Brendan, but I couldn't help telling him it only happened when I taught this little boy who played the same songs Brendan did when he was little.

After working outside for an hour, he came into my piano studio. "I fixed it. The glass was broken in one of the lights, so water was leaking inside of it and shorting the electricity. That's why it was turning off."

He gave me a look, the kind that pierced me, the kind that said: *Do you see? There's a logical reason for everything. You just have to look for it.*

"You don't believe, do you?" I asked him. He shook his head and looked away. I'd learned my logic from him. The five-year plans. The spreadsheets. I was opening up to more now, but I didn't know how to make him believe. He was the skeptic. He said nothing more, but I heard what he meant. *There are no signs. It's not Brendan.*

Jim had that same look now, that same skeptical expression. "Isn't that weird?" I asked him. After a moment, he nodded. "Although," he said, dragging out the word, "it has been pretty cold out. Batteries can die in the cold, especially since you keep your car in the driveway."

"True." I discovered that when I researched car batteries. "But, I always keep my car in the driveway. It's never happened before. And now both of our cars?" Jim's eyebrows raised. He said nothing as he walked away.

I tried pushing away his doubts, but they wound their way inside me. I grabbed a platter of calzones. I brought them downstairs to the boys. I walked around with mimosas, filling glasses, laughing at the stories, pretending this was just another party. But Jim's doubts became mine.

I sounded like an idiot. What's wrong with me?

I kept on smiling, pretending I didn't hear the doubts roaring inside me. *Brendan messing with our cars. Wooden birds in my bag. Songs on the radio. And who do I point to as proof? A medium. Someone who swears he can talk to the dead.*

The party ended an hour later. I endured the goodbyes and the hugs. Michael left to walk the dogs, and the kids ran upstairs to do homework. I trudged back into the kitchen, my legs heavy and tired. Trays of sliders and meatballs lined the countertop. My stomach growled; I hadn't eaten anything during the party.

I placed a few meatballs on a plate. And then I did something I'd feared I would do since that last Tuesday afternoon in August. I forgot. I grabbed the plate and walked to the bottom of the stairs, one hand on the railing, a smile on my face.

Brendan's going to love these meatballs. They were garlicky with just enough breadcrumbs to hold the meat together. This was his favorite time—after a party, when it was all quiet, and we'd pile our plates high with leftovers and sit on the couch, watching TV and eating. He'd talk about the crab legs Aunt Becky brought. We'd laugh about the way Uncle Allan tackled Uncle Jimmy in touch football, and he'd reach for Aunt Patty's cookies, the ones with Hershey Kisses baked inside.

But first, the meatballs. *He's going to love them.* I opened my mouth and called out to him.

"Bren—"

I choked before the second syllable, my hand trailing off the balcony.

He's not upstairs in his room.

He's not downstairs playing video games.

He's not here.

He'll never be here again.

I walked slowly back to the kitchen and threw the meatballs away. I threw away the sliders, the calzones, all the leftovers. I stared at the empty holes in the window screen. They meant nothing to me.

And just like that, the magic was gone.

Caesura

A sudden break in the music, marked on the score with two slashes. It's a silence. And yet there's something there, something that makes me lean toward my piano, listening with every part of my body.

Sometimes, I'll even hold my breath. Waiting. Waiting. It's usually a short pause. The music has so much more to say. The music always returns.

Always.

42

I couldn't stop thinking about fate. There was a time when I thought I didn't believe in it. I sat in high school English class rolling my eyes over the Greek tragedies we studied. No one could outrun their destiny in Sophocles' plays. The Fates were depicted as three women, one who spun the thread of life, another who wove in joy or sorrow, and a third, wielding a scissor, ready to cut the thread of life. I didn't believe in any of it; the idea that someone else controlled my destiny was ridiculous.

And yet so many times in my life I've nodded and said, "It's meant to be."

I said that when Allan brought home his friend from college, and I knew I had met the man I would marry. A year later, Michael knelt on one knee during a carriage ride through Central Park. I flashed my engagement ring at friends, and they gathered round to hear my stories, and each time I finished, I added the words, "It's meant to be," and everyone sighed.

I said those same words when we found our condo in Hoboken. When we moved to the suburbs in New Jersey. When neighbors stood in the street, listening to me play piano and then knocked on my door, asking me to give lessons. Ah, it's meant to be. Each time I said it, I didn't stop to think about God. I didn't listen for the clacking of needles as the sisters of fate wove my destiny.

I said it for sorrows, too. We'd tried for years to get pregnant. Friends opened presents at baby showers, and I wondered when it would be my turn. We finally went to fertility doctors and suffered through months of tests. After the last test, I followed the doctor into his office and before he even said a word, he shook his head and slid a box of tissues across his desk.

"It's not going to happen. Not without medical help," he said. He listed the options, the drugs I could take, the procedures that might allow me to become pregnant. I listened carefully, while panic pounded through me. Maybe it's not meant to be.

The doctor grabbed a pad, ready to prescribe me fertility drugs, but I shook my head. He pushed the prescription slip toward me. I was almost thirty; he didn't want to waste any more time. But I knew we needed to wait. It was October. We'd start after the holidays, in January, a new year, a new life.

Two weeks later, I stood in my bathroom, staring at the positive pregnancy test on the counter. I looked at those two blue lines for a long time, seeing the words, *It's meant to be.*

I held my breath during those early months of my pregnancy, filled with fear over each twinge and cramp. I didn't buy a book or tiny little socks or a bib with a cute saying. I waited until after the fourth month, after we'd heard the swoosh of the baby's heartbeat.

"I don't want to tempt fate," I said. Once, I glanced through a baby book in the store, and then slammed it shut, as if that were enough to stir those sisters into action.

The doctors labeled my pregnancy high risk, but only because of our difficulty in conceiving. Each month our baby grew and we sailed through with no problems. We learned he was a boy and named him Brendan. I painted his room in a wash of sky blue and pasted a border of Winnie the Pooh onto the walls. I bought pregnancy books and stayed up at night, whispering facts to a sleeping Michael, "He can hear today." I started playing him Mozart and Beethoven on my piano, pushing away all thoughts of destiny.

Then, in the seventh month, my blood pressure creeped up and the doctors became concerned I had preeclampsia. They ordered complete bed rest; I was only allowed out of bed for bathroom visits. Michael packed a cooler full of food and water each morning and I stayed on the pull-out bed in the den watching movies and reading books. I couldn't play the piano, but I could sing, and with each lullaby, I rubbed circles on my belly, wondering if this baby was meant to be.

Brendan arrived a few weeks early, healthy and hungry. All my wondering about what was meant to be vanished. He was mine. I didn't think about fate. Or those three women weaving events into my life. Or God, who planned my destiny. I just held him in my arms, knowing he was meant to be.

Can you cheat fate, even when you're not sure you even believe in it? I'd wondered during those years of trying to get pregnant. Maybe I cheated fate when I became pregnant? Or in my seventh month? Or when he was only a few weeks old, and I'd thought I'd lost Brendan.

He slept in the wooden bassinet next to my bed, the same one his Aunt Patty had used for his cousins, Kaitlyn, Jimmy, and Sean. Brendan fell asleep, his mouth curved in that milk smile, moving his lips, sucking gently, already anticipating his next meal. I drifted off, rocked to sleep by the rhythm of those sipping sounds, when suddenly, the silence jerked me awake. I jumped up and looked down at the bassinet. He wasn't there.

I looked at Michael but he was asleep next to me. I looked at the bassinet again. There was a pillow in it. Brendan was under it, his mewls muffled by the pillow. I must have kicked a pillow on top of him in my sleep. I picked him up and moved to the chair in the corner, rocking him for the rest of the night. He was fine, but that image of him suffocating under a pillow haunted me for months.

I'd forgotten about it until fifteen years later when he was gone. What if I were meant to lose him when he was a baby? If I were only supposed to have a few weeks with him instead of fifteen years? I thought of this each time I dragged out the giant sweater box under my bed, the one filled with fifteen years of memories. A friend of mine had lost her baby as a newborn. That could have been me, my box filled only with a blanket and a few baby clothes, a snippet of hair, a wisp of what might have been.

Brendan's box was filled with so much more. The gooey toys he'd loved to stretch and the Legos he'd built and then never played with since he just liked to stare at them. And the coupons; oh how I loved to look at the coupons he'd made me for presents. They weren't just for a kiss or a hug. He'd write things he knew I wanted, like a trip to the bookstore or to watch a decorating show together.

I tried to be grateful for these memories. Maybe Brendan had been given a shorter thread of life, and somehow we stretched it out to last fifteen years until that last Tuesday in August when it finally snapped. It was a hollow victory, though. I wanted to fall down onto my knees and beg the Fates, the universe, God. Anyone. I'd do anything to bargain for an extra inch of his life. His box overflowed with memories, but I wanted more, so much more. I wanted a bigger box.

I ached for one more memory, one more kiss, one more giggle.

I wanted to see the blush bloom across his cheeks the first time he brought home a girlfriend. I wanted to wipe away his tears when his first love shattered. I wanted to hear him blow out a sigh when I took too many pictures at his college graduation, and oh, how I longed for that soft smile on his face when he stared down at his newborn.

43

It was February, cold, dark, and dreary. None of my tricks worked anymore. I couldn't stare at sand, couldn't listen to the songs Michael still brought home. I wrote to Brendan in my journal, sang him a song on the piano. I lit fires in the den and watched the flames for hours. I tried crying under the stars. But that winter, I didn't have the strength or energy to heal my heart. Doubts filled me. Cold settled into my bones.

Even my shadowy harp dreams stopped. I hid my pain and told no one, not even Michael. I still laughed with my kids, still walked with Hedy. And I still went to choir. One Thursday night, I pushed open the wooden doors to the sanctuary. The other choir members were already there, six of them sitting in the pews on the chancel.

"Linda," Argaille sang out as I walked up the steps to the piano. I skirted around the piles of music scattered on the red carpet. Dianne handed me sheets of music. Argaille beamed at me. "I'm so glad you're here." She folded her hands in her lap and sighed deeply. "Let's simmer with this for a moment of appreciation before diving into this educational wonderland of mystical choral waters." She closed her eyes and inhaled deeply, her fingers fluttering by her chest.

Argaille had the ability to hear and knit together many separate voices. This made her a gifted musician. It also made her a little unfocused. Most of the time, I didn't know what she was saying.

I glanced at Dina, my interpreter. She sang my note when I couldn't find the pitch. She moved her hands to the beat and helped me find my way. And when I stumbled over Argaille's flowery words, she leaned forward and whispered an explanation.

"We have new music," she said.

"It's Dump Day," Bruce said, his hands rubbing together. "Anything we don't like, we get to dump."

I smiled at the excitement in his voice. We sang through the new songs, keeping some in our folders, dumping a few onto the ground with a flourish. We moved to a simple communion song.

"That's it," Argaille shouted. "Testify. Let the glory of our voices stack upon each other, each needing the other as we build the splendor."

I glanced back at Dina. "Sing louder," she whispered.

Suddenly, Argaille stopped mid-phrase, her eyes wide as if struck by a new idea. "Linda, why don't you take the next line as a solo?" She played the notes, a simple melody.

I stiffened but nodded. It seemed easy enough. But when it came time to sing alone, my voice cracked. Before, when I sang with the choir, I could hide behind the other voices. But now, my voice sounded so thin I didn't recognize myself. I stopped.

"It's okay," she called out. "I'll start again."

"You can do it," Cheri whispered. Dianne and Laura nodded their encouragement. My hands shook. I squeezed them until my knuckles turned white.

"Find the note, Linda," Argaille trilled. My ears filled with panic instead of the note she pounded. I wanted to touch the note, to reach out and play it on the piano. I felt vulnerable so I reached for my wall, my protection. I'd built it back up this past month. It wrapped around me, surrounding me with strength.

I stood up straight, determined to sing these few notes. I loved singing when I was a child. Outside on my swing, I'd breathe in the earthy smell of my mother's garden, lean back, and pump my feet as the wind brushed through my hair and my giggles turned to laughter. I soared higher and higher until a song burst out of me. I sang folk songs and made-up songs and melodies from Mozart and Beethoven. I flew higher each time until the swing set poles rocked out of place, that hint of danger adding to my exhilaration. I sang and sang, convinced I could touch the sky.

I wanted that now, that feeling of freedom, that childlike belief that I could fly.

"You can do it, Linda," Argaille said. As one, the choir nodded and waited as she played the intro again. I took a breath. My ribs tightened like a vise, squeezing against my diaphragm. I squeaked out a few notes. It sounded like air screeching out of a balloon. I trailed off. Nothing more would come out.

Argaille played the intro again but I shook my head, the lump in my throat blocking the notes inside me. "I can't."

She nodded. "It's okay, dear. Dina will sing it."

She continued to play. I no longer listened. For weeks I'd walked around half asleep, going through the motions, building my wall of ice. It caged the pain. But it also meant that nothing could get out. I couldn't sing. Couldn't find my connection to Brendan. If I wanted that, it meant breaking down my walls and going through the pain. I wasn't sure how to do that or if I were even strong enough to swim in the sorrow.

44

Lizzie and I came home one afternoon to an empty house. I heard the squeak of the trampoline in the backyard. We walked back there and waved at Zack and Michael jumping on the trampoline. It was warm for the beginning of March, the kind of spring day that fills you with hope. Both of them had thrown their jackets over the safety net.

"Careful of your back," I called out. Michael hadn't been on a trampoline in years, but he only winked at me and jumped higher.

"Look at me," Zack said. He flipped in the air and landed on his feet.

Lizzie ran across the grass toward the trampoline, crying, "My turn, my turn." She wiggled out of her jacket and scrambled up the steps.

"Come on," Michael said to me, but I shook my head, pointing to my bad knee. But there was a part of me that wanted to.

"Yeah, Mom, come on," Zack said. I shook my head again, afraid I'd hurt myself.

Lizzie sat in the middle of the trampoline with her arms wrapped around her knees. Zack jumped all around her, trying to make her fall over. It was their game of popcorn. She giggled as her hair flew with each bounce. They started chanting, "Come on, Mom. Come on."

Finally, I shrugged and toed off my shoes. I worried about an injury, but the need to hear their laughter was too strong. I climbed through the safety net.

"Yay," Lizzie said and clapped. Zack bounced higher.

I stumbled and screamed, my fingers still clutching the net. "No one bounce. I need to do this slowly."

The three of them moved to the edge of the trampoline, standing on the bumpers. I walked slowly into the middle and gave a little bounce. My feet barely moved an inch above the trampoline, but I stopped, my arms out to the side, as I wobbled and lost my balance. I took a deep breath.

"Is that it?" Zack asked. Lizzie giggled.

I closed my eyes. I wanted to hear real laughter, not the mocking kind. My knee felt fine, but I was scared. "Give me a minute. It's been a while."

I used to jump on the trampoline when we first bought it. After I put Lizzie down for a nap, the boys and I would climb onto it. We rolled and bounced until we lost ourselves in laughter. But now a little wobble terrified me. I no longer knew how to walk on shaky ground. But I was tired, so, so tired of being scared all the time. I played the piano, but stopped if I saw a neighbor walk by. Even with my windows closed. I couldn't sing a simple solo in choir. *When did I get so afraid?*

I bent my knees and bounced slowly, flying higher with each bounce. The wind whipped my hair up and down, brushing against my cheek.

"Look at Mommy," Lizzie squealed, and I smiled and jumped even higher. I looked up at the dried leaves stuck in the branches of the tree. There were so many times I'd watched Brendan and Zack jump and rip off a leaf, holding it high above their heads like a trophy. A leaf, curled and brown, dangled over the safety net. A yearning grew inside me. A simple one.

I want that leaf.

I wanted to jump into the air with nothing holding me down. I wanted to feel like I could fly again. I grinned and pointed to the leaf. Zack and Lizzie sat down and pounded their fists against the trampoline. "Do it. Do it," they chanted and I sank deep into my knees and pushed off, stretching out my arms. My fingers grazed the leaf, but slid off before I could grab it.

I landed on my butt. My breath whooshed out of me. I ignored Michael's outstretched hand and pushed my palms behind me and bounced back up.

"Are you okay?" he asked.

I didn't look at him. I wasn't worried about breaking something. I wanted that leaf. I needed to do it, to break through my fear and capture my prize. I took a deep breath. "I can do this." I unzipped my jacket and shrugged out of it. I bunched it into a ball and threw it over the net.

I nodded at the kids and Michael and then pointed to the leaf again. I took a deep breath and jumped slowly at first, but then faster, moving my arms in circles, like Zack and Lizzie did before turning a flip. I flew higher with each bounce. I could reach the leaf now, my fingertips grazed it, but still I jumped, feeling as if the wind carried me through the air. I jumped a few more times and then reached for the leaf. I plucked it from the branches, and held it high above me in victory.

"I did it."

Zack and Lizzie clapped and moved into the middle. The extra weight threw me off balance and I fell, rolling into a ball. Lizzie threw herself onto me. I wrapped my arms around her, still holding onto the leaf. Zack and Michael bounced around us while the two of us rolled around. Something shifted inside me. Part of me wanted to shut it down, afraid I would feel too much.

But Zack chanted all around me. *"You did it, Mom! You did it!"* He moved me with each bounce. Lizzie squeezed me tight, her breath tickling against my neck. I was lying on the trampoline, but it still felt as if I were flying in the air, reaching, reaching for something.

"Mom did it!" Zack shouted.

"I did it!" I yelled back. The wall I'd built around my fear shattered.

I was terrified I'd start crying and never stop. But it wasn't tears that burst out of me. It was laughter. It was part scream, part laugh, the kind you can't hold in. Michael froze for a second, uncertain, but then he smiled and threw his head back and laughed with me. It caught hold of the four of us, and we rolled on the trampoline, holding our bellies, laughing until we were breathless and we lay still. I heard the screech of a patio door opening a few houses down. Our neighbor came outside and leaned his hands on his deck railing, looking down at the four of us. He probably wondered if we were laughing or crying.

I opened my fingers to show off the leaf, but it had crumbled. The wind scattered the pieces. Still, I held my hand high. "Look," I said and everyone sat up and stared at my empty hand. There was silence for a moment and then someone started laughing again. I think it was me. We rolled around on the trampoline. Pieces of the leaf bounced around us as we laughed.

I'd forced myself to jump on the trampoline, forced myself to reach for something I wasn't sure I could touch. And the laughter came.

Oh, we had laughed a lot in those early days, but mostly over memories of Brendan. We laughed over the memory of Brendan writing up a legal document over a bet he and Zack had made. Only he deliberately misspelled his name when he signed it. "Sorry," he said with a smug smile when he lost the bet. "That's not how you spell Brendan Broder, so it's not valid in a court of law."

This laughter on the trampoline wasn't about a memory. It wasn't even about Brendan. It just was. It was pure and filled with joy. It poured out of us, as free as flying through the wind.

Grief was a rollercoaster. Something that moved me, something I couldn't control. Brief moments of joy flickered before I was swept away and plunged deep into grief. I thought it was one or the other, either sorrow or laughter.

But now I could bring a spark of light into the darkness. *This is why my mother puts on her lipstick every day.*

I'd believed it was a symbol of strength, her way of coloring away the pain. Part of it was that. But it was more than that. It was her declaration, her manifesto that even when she felt the darkness within, even when she couldn't recognize herself in the mirror, she could still smile and paint her mouth red. It was her way of carrying a tiny piece of joy into her sorrow.

And now I knew that my heart was big enough to carry both the darkness of loss and the light of love.

45

Brendan had a favorite roasting pan, something I used every month or so. It was too big for the kitchen cabinets, so I kept it in the garage. He smiled whenever he saw it on the counter. "Oh, we're having meat tonight." He danced on his toes and rubbed his hands in anticipation. He was fifteen now and no longer marched around the room, chanting, "Meat, meat, meat!" but he was still just as excited. "What's it going to be? A fresh ham? Roast beef? Chicken?"

He loved them all. He hovered by my shoulder, watching as I sprinkled salt and pepper onto the roast beef. I cut slivers of garlic and pressed them into the roast beef. I set the oven high at 450 so the meat would sear into a spice-filled crust, sealing in the juices.

"More garlic," he said and I doubled the amount. "I need more flavor." He nodded when I slid the pan into the oven. I pulled out green beans to snap, but vegetables bored him, so he went into his room to play video games. An hour later, he crept down the stairs, lured by the smell.

"It's not ready," I said as I pulled the roast out of the oven to baste. He didn't care. He pinched off a piece from the top that had already browned. He smelled it and closed his eyes for a second before popping it into his mouth. He sighed with pleasure. "When is it ready? I can't wait."

*

I thought of that day when I went into the garage and reached high and took the pan off the shelf so I could roast a chicken. I hadn't used this pan since the summer. Something slid around the pan. I looked down, my eyes growing wide.

It was another blue bird.

I had a logical explanation for the first bird, even the second one, but I couldn't figure out how this one had gotten inside Brendan's pan. I didn't store the fall decorations in the garage. And even then, the pan was on the third shelf. I picked up a small scrap of wood and threw it onto the cement floor, trying to see if it could bounce that high. I changed the angle, but nothing I did explained how the bird found its way into the pan.

I picked up the bird. The wood pulsed in my palm, the same way the harp in my dreams did. I held it for a long time, swaying to the music only I could hear. For weeks, I'd been living in the darkness. I couldn't believe in anything. Not the birds or the songs or the memories of my dreams. But laughing on the trampoline had loosened something inside me.

I felt something in this wooden bird. And heard the music inside me again. Somehow, this bird was part of the harp. It made no sense. It wasn't logical. And I didn't care.

I walked into the kitchen and grabbed my tote bag and dug out the other two birds. I went upstairs and lined the three of them up on the thick molding of my headboard. I counted them, touching each one, my fingers shaking.

I could no longer hide the birds, not even when Michael stood behind me, his eyebrows raised. "You see?"

I glanced over my shoulder at him. "It's not the birdseed that makes them come," he said. "It's Brendan."

I nodded. For six months, grief had rocked me with so many

different feelings. Overwhelming loss. Fear. Despair. But also wonder and a hint of magic that swirled around me. And now, something else that made me turn toward Michael. A need building inside me that made me shake. It was too strong for me to resist. I held up two fingers. "There's two things, now."

"Only two?"

I smiled slowly. "Oh, it's enough. They're big ones." I reached for the third bird and took a deep breath. "This is going to sound a bit crazy."

Michael grinned. "I like to think that's my specialty."

"You know I was dreaming about a harp."

Michael nodded.

"I felt the wood, even the vibrations around me. I never really saw it. But now?" I held up the new bird. "I think these birds are part of my dream, part of my harp. I can't believe I'm saying this, but in my dreams the birds turn into a harp." I shrugged. "Isn't that strange?"

He shook his head. "It's not strange at all. It's Brendan showing you the way."

I traced the outline of the bird, its curve like the arc of a harp. Its weight was nothing in my hand, but it filled me with strength. And determination. I nodded at Michael. "There's two things. One, I'm ready to rent a harp. Finally. It's time for me to learn how to play. I'm going to make my dream come true."

"Yes," he shouted. "It's about time. I can't wait to hear it in the house. But let's go all in. We'll buy one on Amazon. Maybe it's even Prime." He held up his phone, ready to scroll through harps and buy one with a push of a button.

I shook my head. "It doesn't work like that. I'd never buy an instrument online. I need to play it. Hear it and feel it. Renting one is a good first step."

He shrugged. "But one could be on our doorstep in two days." I looked at him and his shoulders slumped in disappointment. "Okay, you're the musician. You'll rent one. What's the second thing?"

I reached for his hand. "I can't believe I'm saying this. We need to go back to the medium."

He laughed. "I love it."

"Three medium visits in four months? Everyone's going to think we're a bit crazy." But I no longer cared. I held a wooden bird in the palm of my hand, could feel its vibrations flow through me, filling me with an urgency that stripped away all of my defenses. We had to go back to the medium. "Call Glenn. Make an appointment as soon as you can. Now."

I placed the bird onto the headboard and turned back to Michael.

"Now?" he asked. I thought he'd run and make the appointment, but he only stared at me.

"Yes. Now. Do it." I pushed his shoulders. "Now."

He stared at me for a second longer and then bolted out of the room and down the stairs, probably afraid I'd change my mind. I heard the murmurs of his conversation, but I stayed upstairs. The anticipation swelled inside me as I paced circles in my bedroom. With each lap, I stopped and touched the birds, one by one. After a few minutes, he ran back up the stairs, his phone still in his hand. "We have an appointment. Next week. Tuesday."

I let go of the breath I didn't even know I was holding. He walked toward the bed and leaned in close, staring at the three birds on the headboard. He closed his eyes. "I can't believe you found another bird. Thank you, Brendan," he whispered. "Thank you."

We stayed silent for a few moments, until Michael burst out laughing again. He scrolled through the songs on his phone and chose "Hello, It's Me," the one he played whenever he needed a reminder that Brendan was around him. He reached for my hand and spun me around. Everything swirled inside me. The determination. The anticipation. And oh, those sparks of magic lighting the shadows away. We danced until we grew breathless, and still we kept on dancing.

46

It was Tuesday morning. We'd waited until the kids had gone off to school before driving into the city. We arrived a few hours early, so we went to a diner a few blocks from Glenn's apartment building. It was late morning, with only a few people sitting at the counter. "Sit anywhere," the waitress said with a tired wave. We slid into a booth and grabbed some sticky menus. I wasn't hungry, but I ordered French toast and watched while Michael ate his western omelet.

"Do you think he'll come?" he asked again, in between bites.

"He'll come." I reached for the knife and cut the French toast into tiny pieces. It was thick challah, sprinkled with powdered sugar, just as I liked it. I swallowed a piece. It tasted like dust. "He'll come."

Michael dug back into his omelet. I put my fork down. It was my feeling when I'd found the third wooden bird that made us come here today. I didn't hear actual words, more like a knowing that hummed inside me. But fear made me doubt myself. The last time we'd visited Glenn, we left with magic swirling all around us. It gave us a sense of peace that helped us survive the holidays. It made us think we could find a way forward. We had hope. I didn't want today to shatter that. All because I found a little wooden bird and had a feeling.

I swirled the bits of bread through a puddle of syrup, tracing designs on my plate until Michael finished eating and it was time to go. He signaled for our check.

I stood up. "Let me just wash my hands. They're all sticky."

When I came back, Michael had already put a few dollars and some change on the table for a tip. He stood up and rubbed his hands together. "Okay, let's go."

I reached for my coat and then stopped. I stared at the table.

"What's wrong?"

"Nothing."

But I couldn't look away from the pile of coins. *Pennies.* I slid three of them closer to me. "I feel something with these pennies. Weird." I picked them up, one by one, and put them into my palm. I flipped them over, expecting to see Brendan's birth year on them. Or something that made me think of him. But the year on them was 2011. I bent over them, squinting, trying to find something that connected them to Brendan. They felt warm in my palm, heavier than pennies.

"What is it?"

"Nothing." I frowned. "There's nothing on them. I thought for sure—" I shook my head.

"Well, there's another one on the table." He leaned over, reaching for the other penny.

"No," I said, almost shouting. "They have to be shiny pennies. I don't know why." I tucked the three shiny pennies into my pocket, their warmth filling me, giving me strength. I took a deep breath. "Okay, I'm ready."

We walked the few blocks in silence, the cold breeze stinging my eyes. The bite of French toast was a rock inside my stomach. But as we neared Glenn's apartment, my steps became lighter until it felt as if I were floating. I stopped and grabbed Michael's arm.

"He's here." I'd promised Michael he'd come, never telling him the doubts that weighed me down. But now, the wind wrapped around us, filling every part of me. We stood on the street, our breaths mingling together. We inhaled deeply, breathing in our son. "He's here. C'mon."

I tugged on his arm, pulling him up the steps to Glenn's building. The last time, we'd hesitated, fear freezing us on his doorstep. But now, I wanted to run up the steps and into his apartment. *He's here. Hurry.*

Michael rang the doorbell. It buzzed back. We pushed into the small foyer, laughing as we almost tripped over each other. The wind slammed the front door shut. *Hurry.* I grabbed the wooden banister. Michael didn't need it. I raced up the stairs after him. Before we even got to the first landing, Glenn poked his head out over the stairs. We moved faster. Two more flights to go.

"Hello," he called down. "I knew it was you guys. I remember you from a few months ago. Your son is here already." Michael gasped and took the stairs two at a time. I stumbled a bit on the next landing, but I didn't stop. It felt like Brendan pushed me from behind.

Hurry.

Michael ran up the last few stairs and then reached for my hand, pulling me up and into the hallway. Glenn smiled at us. "Your son came while I was meditating, getting ready for your appointment." We stood outside his door now, breathing hard.

"He's very impatient," Glenn said and we laughed. That's Brendan. Always impatient. "He kept saying, 'My parents are coming. My parents are coming.'"

Michael's fingers crushed my hand.

"Come on in," Glenn said and opened his door wide. We took a step inside. "He's so excited. He has so much he wants to say to you."

I know. It was like a shout inside me. Brendan wanted us there.

Glenn pointed to the molding above the door. "He asked me to do something while we were waiting. That rarely happens. He told me to take pennies and place them above my door."

"Pennies?" I asked. I looked up, trying to catch a glimpse of them.

"Shiny pennies," Glenn said as he closed the door. "He said they could only be shiny pennies."

Michael and I looked at each other. "I told you," he said. "You know what he's saying. You can feel what he wants you to know. You just have to trust it."

We moved inside and sat down at the table. Everything was the same from months before. The glass of water. The candle. The last time we were here, I'd grabbed Glenn's arm at the end of the session. "I wish I could hear him like you do," I said.

"But you can," he answered. "All you have to do is listen within. Then you will hear him." At the time, I didn't believe him. But I was no longer the same person who'd walked into his apartment a few months before. I wasn't waiting for Brendan to come through. He was already here; I felt him in every part of me.

Glenn started the reading. I nodded each time he spoke and gave us an image of Brendan. I didn't analyze or try to find the logic. I simply nodded my head and thought, *Yes, I know.*

"His energy is all around you. He comes like a bird." I nodded, seeing the birds clinging to my window screen and the wooden ones lined up on my headboard. *I know.*

"He's in a car now. He likes to say hello to you guys in the car. He has the keys in his hand." Glenn hunched over, his wrist turning keys, as if trying to start the car. "It won't start. He's laughing now. Saying he's sorry. He wasn't messing with you, just saying hello."

I looked over at Michael, thinking of all those car batteries we'd bought.

Glenn pointed to the Beatles poster above him. "He loves music now, especially Chopin." He tilted his head, listening. "Wait, he wants me to play you a song." He grabbed his phone and started typing. "Yes, here it is." He pressed play and I started smiling. It was Chopin's Nocturne, Op. 72, No. 1. It was a haunting melody, composed after his sister's death. I'd played it just the night before, feeling Brendan and the blend of beauty and sorrow.

Michael glanced at me. "This is the song I keep playing," I said.

He nodded. "Of course it is."

I felt the final notes of the song settle inside me. Glenn turned off his phone and then tilted his head and listened. "He's playing the piano again, but he has a new favorite instrument."

He stopped and Michael leaned forward. "What is it?"

I knew, of course. I'd been dreaming about it for months. The rental was coming later that afternoon. Glenn smiled and plucked the air in front of him. "A harp. This one is a small one. He's holding it in his hands." I almost turned around as if I could see what Glenn saw.

I'd see nothing, but it didn't matter. I could feel it. I felt the wood beneath my palms and the strings trembling beneath my fingers. Michael reached for my hand, squeezing tight. Glenn took a sip of water, staring at the air behind him, listening to Brendan's words. He nodded. "He wants you to play the harp."

I felt the pennies in my pocket, a little zing reminding me that I knew all of this. The birds. The car battery. The harp. The first time we'd come here, after Glenn had given us images of Brendan, I was terrified that we'd somehow lose Glenn. That he would move away and I'd lose my only connection to my son. But those pennies, my feelings, hummed inside me. It's magic swirled all around me. I no longer needed Glenn to give me these messages. I could feel them for myself.

I smiled. "Yes. I know."

47

Later that afternoon, my harp arrived. I'd signed a three-month rental contract from a teacher a few towns away. She was a tiny woman, dwarfed by the harp as she wheeled it into our house and into my living room.

She tuned it, all forty strings. I didn't ask any questions, just watched, knowing I'd google how to tune later. She moved through each string, leaning in as she listened to the notes. Finally, she sat up straight and played a song, her fingers flying over the strings. There was more power in the notes than I expected and yet a gentleness. She played her last note, her hand floating midair as she looked around the room.

"This is a beautiful teaching studio."

I nodded, not wanting to answer her, suddenly terrified she'd ask me to play the piano. I could now play with the windows open, even when neighbors walked by, but my stomach tensed at the idea of playing in front of another musician.

She played a final arpeggio and then handed me the tuning key. "I hope you enjoy it." I waited until she drove away before I turned back to the room. I still hadn't touched the harp, had barely looked at it. It was taller than me, with blond natural wood. I traced the flutes carved into its column. I tapped each of the seven pedals with my foot.

"Well?"

Michael, Zack and Lizzie stood at the doorway. Michael had his eyebrows raised, waiting for me to say, yes, this is it.

I wrapped my arms around the wood. "It's beautiful."

"Look at the strings," Lizzie said. "I thought they were all white, but some are colored."

I laughed. I touched the middle red string. "All the red ones are Cs, the black ones, Fs."

Zack moved into the room. "Can I try?"

I grinned. "Me first."

I sat down and pulled the harp to me, resting it on my shoulder, in between my legs. I'd watched so many videos on how to sit behind one. It had seemed awkward to balance it, but this felt natural, as if I'd done it for years. I reached out and placed my finger on the D string.

"Ready?"

Lizzie nodded. I plucked the string, pulling my finger back into my palm just like I'd seen. The note floated up, toward the vaulted ceiling. I played all the Ds. Lizzie shivered. "Ooh. It's beautiful," she whispered. "It sounds like church."

She was right. It sounded like it belonged in church. I plucked out a series of notes, picking out a simple melody.

"Wow," Michael said. "You can already play a song."

"Well, just with one hand. And I'm using the same finger. It's going to take a while to get the technique down."

"Don't overdo it," he warned.

My injuries were so much better, but he knew I wanted to play for hours. "Don't worry, I'm only going to play for ten minutes."

Zack went upstairs, and Michael and Lizzie went into the kitchen to make dinner. I turned back to the harp, hugging it to me. I rested the soundboard against my chest and plucked notes that flowed right through me. I forced myself to stop after fifteen minutes. I rocked the harp back into standing position and walked into the kitchen, my hands out in front of me. I wiggled my fingers.

"Are you okay?" Michael asked.

"Yeah. No pain. But it's weird. It feels like pins and needles. Only better." My fingers still tingled from the vibrations. "I know I've only played for a few minutes, but I have a feeling this is going to heal my elbow and wrists. Maybe even my thumbs. I think my fingers are going to get really strong." I stretched them out and shrugged. "Either that, or completely destroy them."

Michael looked at me, and I smiled, knowing all the unspoken questions he wanted to ask. *Is this it? Is this your dream? Are you happy?*

I couldn't answer him. Not yet. It felt different to me, the wood beneath my palms. It sounded beautiful, and I loved playing it, but I wasn't sure yet if this was the harp of my dreams.

That night, I placed the three shiny pennies above my door frame. They were hidden, something I couldn't see when I looked up, but a message I could feel. Perhaps the pennies were what pulled me out of sleep that night.

It was two in the morning. The house was silent, but I crawled out of bed, moved by music only I could hear. I crept downstairs and stood by the harp. I put my hand on the wood, feeling the vibrations. I didn't play, not even a gentle melody, but still, I felt the sound all around me, my son moving through me. After a few minutes, I went back upstairs and fell asleep.

The next day, I texted Michael and told him about waking in the middle of the night, and how strongly I'd felt Brendan. I ended my text with the line: *He was with me.*

He texted me back: *You felt him strongly when you looked at cruises?*

I squinted at my phone, confused. I'd said nothing about a cruise, only about feeling Brendan in the harp. I was about to ask him what he was talking about, but the dogs barked and scratched at the front door. When I came back from the walk, there was another text waiting for me.

Just so you know, I'm ready to start looking.

I texted him back: *Looking for what?*

His answer: *I think I can do a cruise now.*

It took us a while to figure out what we were talking about, that somehow, Michael had received a different message than the one I'd texted him. When he came home that night, we discovered my phone showed the text I'd sent about the harp and feeling Brendan in the middle of the night. But that's not the message that ended up on his screen. His text was the one about a cruise I had sent months before, only now it ended with an additional line, one taken from my new text: *He was with me.*

It wasn't autocorrect. We stared at the two phones and their two different messages. "Brendan texted us," Michael whispered. "He took both your texts and combined them." He shook his head, but not because he didn't believe. His voice was filled with awe. I didn't know how to answer; this was something logic could never explain. But it didn't matter. The line between hope and insanity had vanished. I held my phone to my heart and believed.

He yelled for the kids. Zack and Lizzie came running and then gasped when they saw our phones and the two different messages. The dogs barked and danced at our feet.

"Brendan texted us," Michael shouted.

"He's so strong," Glenn had said only the day before. "And really good with electronics. He reads the texts his brother and sister still send him. He's strong enough to text back. He won't, of course. Then they'd never stop texting him. They'd be staring at their phone all day, waiting for him." Glenn picked up his phone off the table and held it up. "But he's strong enough to use this. He knows how to pierce the veil between our worlds. He's even teaching his grandfather how to send signs. This kid is really strong."

Pride swelled inside me as I pictured Brendan showing his Papa Ben what to do. *That's my Brendan.* But I couldn't let go of the idea that he could text us. "One text would be nice," I said.

Glenn laughed. "Maybe. But he won't. He's sending you enough signs through music and birds."

I looked down at my kitchen table now, with both of our phones side by side. We couldn't stop staring at it.

"He heard Glenn," I whispered as the kids yelled about a cruise going to Alaska. "It was like a dare for him."

A challenge. Brendan could never resist a challenge.

I smiled, seeing Brendan standing behind Glenn, his arms crossed, a smirk curling his lips. He raised his eyebrows when Glenn held up the phone and said Brendan would never use it. I could almost hear Brendan laughing. "You think I won't use the phone?"

He rubbed his hands together and then nodded once. "Challenge accepted."

We booked the trip that weekend. We'd be in Alaska in July for Brendan's sixteenth birthday. It would be more than just a vacation. I'd find something there, something Brendan wanted me to find.

Maybe peace. And yes, surrounded by trees frosted with snow, the four of us would find a measure of peace. It would seep into our souls and wrap us in comfort.

But there was something more. Something I could hold in my hand and take home with me. It stirred excitement inside me. I wasn't sure what it would be, but there was something Brendan meant for me to find in Alaska.

48

I grew bold. I played the harp and kept my windows open, not even stopping when a neighbor walked by. I invited Zack and Lizzie into the room so they could hear me play a song. The dogs ran into the living room each time they heard my opening glissando. They curled up on the rug beside me and closed their eyes, lulled by the music.

I played for hours each day. I loved its sound and the way my arms ached and the tingling in my fingers. But something felt different. This harp wasn't mine. It was just a rental. I no longer dreamt of harps, but I remembered the way the wood had felt. My hand still felt the shape of its curve and the way the strings vibrated beneath my fingers. This harp was beautiful, but it wasn't mine. I still had time left on the rental contract, but it didn't matter; I couldn't wait. I needed to buy the harp of my dreams.

The four of us drove three hours to a store that sold only harps. I'd bribed the kids with the promise of eating in a nearby diner that served dozens of different types of grilled cheese sandwiches. I squinted through the tinted window of the store, disappointed that it seemed so dark. I'd expected lights and a big harp sign written in golden letters. I anticipated music piped out onto the sidewalk, a series of glissandos that overlapped each other. Anything that made me think *Yes, this is it.*

"Don't touch anything," I said to Zack and Lizzie before we walked into the narrow storeroom. The store wasn't the kind of place made for browsing; an appointment was needed just to walk through the doors.

Harps stood in rows on the floor and hung on the wall, a medley of small lap ones and giant gilded ones that belonged in a king's palace. I felt a little dizzy, surrounded by so many strings that shimmered in the light. I itched to run my fingers over the harps. I put my hands behind my back.

Michael greeted the saleswoman while I stood there, over-whelmed. I wasn't sure how to ask which one might be my dream. She sensed my hesitation.

"Let me play a few harps for you," the woman said. She was tall, with long hair that danced across her back as she played. I'd spoken with her a few days before. I told her nothing about myself, only that I was a pianist and wanted to learn a new instrument.

She played a quick song on the first harp and then moved her bench to another one. On the fourth harp, she stopped suddenly and smiled at the look on my face. "Yes," she said as she stood up. "You play the piano. I knew you'd want a pedal harp."

I'd told Michael that was what I wanted before we even walked through the door. The rental at home was a small pedal harp. They were more money than a lever harp, more like buying a car. But its sound was bigger and its pedals allowed for more notes. As a musician, I didn't want to be limited. I wanted to play with all the colors.

She waved at the bench, an invitation I couldn't resist. I ran my fingers down the fluted column and traced the gilded scrolls on the soundboard. I sat down, pulling the harp toward me until it balanced midair and barely rested on my shoulder. Wrapping my arms around it, I plucked a few strings, my fingers pulling into my palm. I loved its bright and full sound, strong enough to sing alongside a symphony. Zack saw my smile and nudged Lizzie with his elbow. It wasn't a *Yay, Mom found her harp* nudge. This was more like, *Yay, now we get to go to the diner.*

I played a scale with my left hand, feeling the bass notes echo inside my chest. My fingers shook. The kids stared at me, waiting. Michael gave me an expectant look and I raised my eyebrows at him, my code for *I think I found it.* It was a beautiful instrument. I'd have fun exploring its many different colors.

But when I stood up, I noticed a black Celtic harp the next row over. It was a floor harp like the one I'd just played, but so much smaller. I ignored Zack's disappointed face and walked toward it, my steps slowing as I neared. The top of its arch barely reached my chin. I touched it gently, my hand trailing over the curve of black wood and resting on the light-colored soundboard. It was plain, with no carvings or gilded scrolls. It felt warm, as if I'd just spent hours playing it, just like in my dreams. I wanted to hear its sound, needed to hear its voice, but my fingers trembled too much to place them on the strings.

"Can you play me something?" I asked the clerk. She nodded and carried the bench over. She sat down. I held my breath as she played and listened to the sound of Ireland and green rolling hills, shivering as if wind and rain poured down on me. As she played, the magic moved inside me. The pedal harp I'd just played had power and presence, but the gentle voice of this Celtic harp tore me apart.

She kept playing, and its soft sound weaved itself inside me. No melody had played in my harp dreams, only vibrations that washed over me. This was the same feeling. It filled me, pushing against my heart, and yet it left me broken. This was my dream.

She finished her song and saw the tears streaming down my face. I'd told her nothing about Brendan, nothing about my dreams, but she nodded as if she had been waiting for my tears.

I nodded back. "This one," I whispered. "This is the one I want."

I didn't play it. After all these months of yearning, I didn't play it. My fingers trembled too much. I'd never bought an instrument before without playing it, but this was the one for me, the one I'd been playing in my dreams for months now.

The clerk took it into the back to tune it and I paced the storeroom, waiting. The kids went out onto the sidewalk. I could hear their argument over french fries or onion rings. Michael ran outside with the case to make sure it would fit in the trunk of the car. I wasn't worried; we'd find a way for the harp to fit.

"Are you sure?" he asked right before we paid. His eyes were worried. He'd seen my tears, seen the way my hands still shook. I knew what he was thinking: *Why would she choose the harp that made her cry instead of the one that made her smile?*

Yes, this harp held sorrow. I still felt its vibrations flowing inside me, pushing against the hurt, making it ache even more. It would be so easy to say no to this harp and protect myself from pain.

I could take home the pedal harp, the one whose sound filled the room but left my heart alone. That would be the easy choice. But I needed to follow my dreams. It had to be this one. I needed to pull it toward me and wrap my arms around it. If I leaned into the ache, if I pressed it against my heart, someday, somehow, this harp would heal me.

I squeezed Michael's hand. "This is it."

49

I tried not to sound crazy when friends asked me how I was doing.
"I'm doing okay," I said. "Really."

"I'm learning to play the harp," I offered as proof.

I wanted to show them the calluses, to flash them the tiny scars the strings had imprinted on my fingers. They were shaped like half-moons and seemed to shine in the darkness.

"Can you see them?" I asked friends and family. I held my fingers in front of their faces, angling them to catch the light, but I was the only one who could see them.

My scars were like the strings on my harp. When I plucked a string, it vibrated so fast that it seemed to disappear for a few seconds. If I wanted to play that same string again, I couldn't reach out with a tentative touch. That would make it buzz. I learned how to reach for an invisible string with confidence.

Each morning, I sat behind my harp and pulled it toward me. It seemed to wobble as I rocked it back to rest against my shoulder, its front legs lifted. This was my favorite part of playing, this moment of instability. I pulled the wood toward me until it became part of me, and yet it barely touched me as it balanced in the air.

The harp is an ancient instrument, crafted thousands of years ago. I think part of its fascination lies in its contradictions. It seemed so delicate, ethereal, and yet, over a thousand pounds of force pressed and pulled against its wooden frame.

I played all thirty-four strings spanning the range. I swayed forward, reaching to pluck the long bass strings with my left hand. The notes lingered inside my chest. I leaned back for the high soprano notes with my right hand, playing notes that twinkled for a second before disappearing.

In ancient times, harpists were hired by kings once they'd proven they could evoke three things from their audience: tears, laughter, and dreams. Tears were the easiest. They flowed each time I played.

Most days, I started with an Irish ballad, a simple melody meant as a prayer. My arms wrapped around the wood, my fingers resting on strings. They were nylon and a bit slippery, but the calluses only I could see held me in place. I wore socks so my feet could feel the whisper of notes through the wooden floor.

The notes drifted around me, like wind chimes twirling in the breeze. I closed my eyes and smiled at its peaceful sound. But then, I reached up and flipped down a few of the levers, loosening some of the strings, shifting into a minor key. A darkness washed over the notes, a low rumble of thunder that brought the rain. The song moved from prayer to lament. I let my tears take over.

When I was young, we had an oil lamp in our living room. Inside it was a statue of a woman sitting in a garden, surrounded by strings, with drops of oil dripping down each one. She looked as if she were crying, trapped within a cage of rain. Was that how I looked each time I played, trapped within these strings, the tears flowing down?

But I wasn't trapped by tears. A simple shift of my levers and my notes brightened. I was surprised how quickly I found laughter within my strings. I rolled a chord, each finger curling into my palm, one at a time, but moving so quickly it looked like one motion. The sound rippled against me, like a wave. I rolled another chord and then another, because here in these four notes was my son. It was his giggle when you tickled him underneath his chin and his snort whenever Michael made a stupid joke.

How Brendan loved to laugh. I searched for that sound. My fourth finger of my left hand reached for the bass notes. My arm moved in circles, rising and falling as I built the rhythm. *One, two, three. One, two, three.* The beat became a bounce that spread throughout the house, like a call that beckoned.

I looked up and saw Michael standing in the doorway, smiling as he wiggled his eyebrows. He entered the room, arms stretched wide, his toes tapping against the wooden floor. My fingers fluttered a trill of high notes, like birds chirping in the trees, and he moved faster, twirling as he made up his own Irish jig.

"More," he said and leapt across the room. He pranced around me, his hands on his hips, his legs kicking to the beat. Together, we braided our laughter into the song. Lizzie came running and tapped her feet in time to her daddy's dance. I slowed down the tempo, just a bit. She climbed on top of his feet, and they held hands and waltzed across the room, counting *one, two, three, one, two, three.*

Zack stuck his head into the room, lured by the laughter, but then backed away, red staining his cheeks. He was too embarrassed to dance. He couldn't even watch us. But later that night, there was a rhythmic thump coming from his bedroom. I stood in his doorway and watched as he sat on his bed, propped up by pillows, his eyes closed. He kicked his feet in time, hitting the wall, and I counted the *one, two, three* from the song I'd played earlier. He hummed the melody, a soft smile on his face. He felt me watching him and opened his eyes.

He shrugged and looked away, but he couldn't stop his laughter from spilling out. We gave in to it, still hearing the music that only played inside us. It reached deep within. It pulled and lifted us, until the whole house was filled with our laughter.

50

E ven the birds loved to listen to me play the harp. It was April now, and they'd returned, hanging on to my window screens. I played for them, and it seemed as if they bobbed their beaks in time. I bought a bird book and learned to recognize the orange-bellied red robin and the muddy-brown feathers of a wren. There were so many birds I couldn't tell apart, but it didn't matter. It wasn't the flash of yellow or blue that called to me; it was the sound of their song.

I listened online to chirps and trills until I could make out their different calls when they spoke to me during the day. I could hear the jeer of the blue jay and the whispery *peter peter* of the tufted titmouse and the siren of a cardinal swooping through a dozen notes.

They knocked on my back door, inviting me to play.

I answered their invitation and carried my harp outside on the deck. *Outside.* For the first time, I played outside, not caring that the neighbors could hear. It was the backyard, where I could see no one, but still, it was outside.

I listened to the birds, to their songs, trying to copy their melodies. I researched and discovered that all birds use calls to communicate, but it's the male bird that sings the song. It takes energy to sing, so the song is proof of stamina. It warns predators away and showcases his skill. The song becomes seduction, a calling card for a future mate to admire before she even meets him.

I tried playing their songs, but there were too many. Some had a repertoire of more than two hundred songs. The father bird has only a few months before his young fly away; that's enough time for him to sing the songs that will live inside them. He trains his son to repeat his patterns. He lulls his daughter with song until the melody imprints upon her heart. It becomes her soul song. This is how she will choose her mate: she listens and waits until she hears the echo of her father's song.

I played for the birds that knocked on my back door, surrounded by trees springing back to life. I pretended it was only the birds that could hear me. Sometimes, I thought they answered me back. Oh, I knew most of their calls were logistic. A whistle warning others about the red-tailed hawk flying above or the bubble of chirps that invited friends to share their seed.

I listened, knowing that mixed within all these sounds, a bird was singing a special song. He sang the song taught to him by his father, knowing his melody was etched within the heart of another. He's like the sparrow who tapped on my door, the one Michael cradled in his hands. He's not sure if she was listening, or if she's even out there. Still, he sang, hoping one day she would hear. He sat in his tree and sang his song of love, waiting to be remembered.

I played. I wanted an echo, the call of my son. I heard nothing and yet, there was something in the silence. A waiting that filled me with excitement. We were leaving for Alaska in a few months. Perhaps that was what made me lean in and feel a rhythm pulse inside me, a drumbeat of anticipation as I listened for the song of my son.

51

I stood in front of the piano at my church. Michael and the kids were sitting with the congregation, but I was so scared, I couldn't look at them. I held music in my hand. The music had fallen twice now. Each time I placed it on the piano, my hands shook so much it slid down to the floor. It was the last time the choir would sing together before summer break.

Argaille had broken her hip a few weeks before. She'd fallen in the vestibule at church and before the ambulance had even pulled into the hospital, she called and left a message on my phone: *I need you to accompany the choir.* I stood in my kitchen and listened to the message three times, trying to slow my breath down. She called again before I could listen for the fourth time.

Over six months before, I'd talked to her on the phone while holding the slip of paper where Michael had written the word *Courage.* I'd believed it was a gift from Brendan. The memory of that made me say yes to her request, but now, standing in the church, waiting for the choir to walk in, I couldn't even put the music on the piano.

"Are you okay?" Dina asked. Her voice was quiet; I could barely hear her above the pounding in my head. I held up the music shaking in my hands, "Peace Like a River."

The song had a gospel feel to it, with thick chords and grace notes that sounded like water rippling over rocks. I'd done fine a few days before at rehearsal, but now my fingers wouldn't work. Dianne had helped me tape the pages together accordion style, like Argaille did, so I could turn the pages quickly. But my fingers couldn't even hold onto the paper.

Bruce and Bob walked into the back pew. The sopranos—Dianne, Cheri and Laura—filed into the front one next to the piano. They stayed standing, ready to sing. Cheri nodded at me; she was my cue-giver, the one who guided me when to stand and when to sit. I slid onto the piano bench, still holding the music.

She tilted her head again. *It's time.*

I took a deep breath. Dina reached over and steadied the paper. "I'll turn for you," she said and stood behind me instead of standing with the choir. She placed her hand on my shoulder and started to sway, her choir robe flowing with the beat. Even with my eyes on the music, I could sense her movement, like a living metronome. I waited until I could feel her pulse beat inside me. Through the open window, I could hear a few birds chirping. Their song calmed my nerves a bit. Perhaps I could play the piano for the birds.

I waited another few seconds until their song was louder than my fear. Finally, I nodded at the choir. My fingers sank into the opening chords.

There's a moment in a song when I need to let go. I'd learned the notes, had practiced slowly with a metronome and then with the choir. I knew the chord progressions, when the key signature changed. My muscles had memorized this song. If I played it the way I'd trained, I'd be fine. I'd hit all the right notes and rhythm, but the music needed more than that. *Feel your music.* That's what I told my piano students. *Let go and feel the music.*

I played the introduction, trying to sink into the song and the pull of Dina's hand marking time. I wanted the music to flow through me like it did at home, when I could feel the story of the song. But I held back, afraid to feel. If I soared with the music, I might shatter my control and collapse into a sobbing heap.

Dina moved to the side of me. Her presence calmed me, as her alto voice filled the church. I began to sway on the bench, rocking back and forth as I reached for chords in the bass. I played for the birds, and the music slowly took over. Her hand moved to the beat, and I rocked with her, slipping into the story I imagined. I stood on a rock, the river teasing my toes, the spray of water cooling my face. In the distance, through the mist, I saw a shadow. *Brendan.*

He stood on the bank of the river, waiting for me to cross to the other side. He didn't wade into the waters to help, not even when the song swelled and the water reached my knees.

My breath grew ragged, but still I played. My right hand mirrored the melody the sopranos sang, a whirlpool of notes that almost pulled me under. I kept playing. Bruce sang the harmony, a deep bass line that steadied me. I'd learned to listen for his voice to guide me through the song. It steadied me now as I moved through the water. Each time my left hand played a chord, I imagined stepping to another rock. I held my breath for that small leap of faith as I pushed through, searching for the next rock. I moved closer to Brendan.

The choir crescendoed. Bob's voice rang out, reminding me it was his voice that had made me want to sing with the choir. My fingers stumbled on the keys. I wanted to stop, needed to stop before I drowned. But Brendan stood on the bank. Smiling. Waiting. He crooked his arm and nodded at me. And I remembered the nights last year, when the muscles around my knee had failed, and I needed help climbing the stairs. The kids would fight over who could help me, but Brendan was the only one strong enough to bear my weight.

He wouldn't stand next to me on the stairs, but instead stood on the step above, waiting. He was usually so impatient, moving as fast as he could, but not when he stood on the staircase to help me. He crooked his elbow, his fist closed. He stiffened his arm until it was solid. He didn't pull me up each step—didn't help me at all— not even when my knee buckled and I wobbled. He said nothing, only offered his arm so I could grab hold and steady myself, waiting until I could pull myself up.

That's what he was doing now, with the choir singing and this river raging all around me. I could feel him standing there, in the distance, his arm held out, waiting for me to cross over the river. I tried to lose myself back in the song. I glanced to my left and saw Bob standing straight, his face serious as he sang. I listened to all the parts stacked together, their voices blending.

I rocked back and forth on the piano bench, reaching for the octaves, feeling the music flow inside me. Tears welled in my eyes, blurring my notes, but I didn't stop. Each measure I played moved me one rock closer to Brendan waiting across the river. I played some grace notes, quick notes that slid into the next, pinpricks of light in the mist showing me the way. I moved closer, one rock at a time, letting the music pull me, until I played the final chords and climbed onto the river bank. I reached out for Brendan. My hand wrapped around his arm and I breathed in his strength, until it trembled inside my bones.

I did it.

Dina leaned in close, her hands on my shoulders. "He's always with you," she whispered. I nodded. I'd heard that so many times. I'd felt Brendan before; sometimes, I even knew what he wanted me to know. But this was the first time I believed that it would be enough. I stood up and smiled at the choir. I wanted to throw my arms wide, like Michael did when he received a message from Brendan. I wanted to shout my gratitude. I'd played what I felt inside, even when it was a brokenness that took my breath away. This was a gift from God. Or maybe Brendan. I wasn't sure if I could tell the difference anymore.

It didn't matter. I let my music out. I reached for something in the mist, something I couldn't really see. I held onto both Brendan and God. I didn't push away the divine. I let its mystery wrap around me and settle between the cracks of my heart.

It was enough.

52

There were too many feathers in Seattle. The four of us were walking along the wooden boardwalk overlooking the Puget Sound. The next day we'd board the ship for our cruise to Alaska. We'd spent the day at the aquarium watching dolphins dance and twirl for fish treats. Then we walked to Pike Place Market and waited in line for giant crepes smothered with chocolate and strawberries.

"Look, Mama! Another one," Lizzie cried and bent down to pick up a feather. "When feathers appear, angels are near." She held it up, running her finger along its gray edge, before placing it in her other hand. She'd been collecting them all day, believing each one to be a sign from Brendan, like scattered breadcrumbs showing us the way.

She still lived in a world of fairytales, where frogs transformed into princes, and straw spun into gold. She still believed in Santa and left long letters for the tooth fairy. Perhaps logic might have started creeping in, especially if older brothers started whispering doubts to her.

But when Brendan died, she pushed away all her questions. She fell under the spell of butterflies and the birds that still knocked on our door. She believed in feathers and the magic of her brother.

Suddenly, Lizzie laughed. "Look at this one," she said and held up one as long as her forearm. She nudged Zack, trying to make him jealous.

"Who cares?" Zack asked. "Atta wee. Get wrecked." He waved his hands up and down in front of his face as he said the nonsense taunt. It usually riled her up, but she only shrugged and skipped away, her eyes cast down, searching for more feathers.

In the distance, we saw lights twirling in the sky.

"It's a Ferris wheel," Zack said, pointing ahead. "Can we go on it?"

"Sure," Michael said before I could shake my head no.

Lizzie handed me her feathers, and the two of them ran toward the line. The Ferris wheel seemed to stretch into the clouds and swing out over the water. It scared me.

"I'll stay here," I said as we moved closer to the Ferris wheel. Michael bought the tickets, and the three of them climbed into the gondola. My stomach lurched when it swayed. It wasn't so much the height, but the uncertainty of the gondola, the way it swung each time someone shifted their weight. I needed something solid under me.

The wheel spun around. I waved each time they came around again, making sure to smile. The ribs of the feathers dug into my palm, but I welcomed the small pain, hoping it would calm my queasiness. They ran up to me a few minutes later.

"That was awesome," Zack said and gave me a high five.

"It felt like we could touch the clouds," Lizzie said.

I laughed. "It looked like it from here." I handed her the feathers back and we started walking to our hotel. Michael waited until the kids were ahead of us.

"Are you okay?" he whispered. "You look a little pale."

"It's hard for me to watch you guys up so high."

He laughed. "How are you going to get on the seaplane in a few days?"

I shrugged. It was months ago when we'd booked expeditions for our cruise in Alaska. I'd spent days researching. I didn't want bus tours or shopping trips; I wanted something unique. Adventurous. I'd been filled with anticipation and a feeling I was meant to soar.

"Let's fly over the glaciers in a seaplane," I'd said.

Michael had raised his eyebrows. "Are you sure?"

"Yes." We'd booked that and a helicopter ride that landed on a glacier where dogs trained to pull a sled.

I didn't expect to feel sick months later, watching my family climb onto a ride less than two hundred feet high. The seaplane would fly much higher than that. I took a deep breath, letting it out slowly. Lizzie chased a feather floating in the wind, laughing when she snatched it in the air.

"This is the best one yet."

She held her feathers like a bouquet of magical flowers. I wanted to grab them, to take hold of their magic, but I was filled with fear. How could I climb onto that airplane? I couldn't even watch my family on a Ferris wheel. There was no way I'd be able to soar high into the sky.

A few days later, we stood on the wooden pier in Juneau, waiting for our turn to board the seaplane. We'd already seen a safety video in a little shed lined with life preserver jackets. I winced when they told us everyone had a window seat; I wanted to be squished inside a wall of people.

The kids were excited, and so I kept my face calm, nodding each time Lizzie pointed out a seagull or Zack skipped a rock across the water. The seaplanes on the water bobbed up and down like toys. I wasn't sure if I could get on one of them. I wasn't even sure if I could inch closer to the pier, to stand on the platform that rocked up and down from the waves.

Michael scanned the skies for an eagle. The guide had told him they rarely come because of the noise from the planes and the restaurants lining the waterfront. Still, he strained each time he saw a bird, hoping it was an eagle.

A family boarded a plane and we took a big step forward. I begged Brendan to give me strength. Or send me a sign that I should walk away and spend the day buying tacky souvenirs.

"Look, there's an eagle," Michael shouted. He fumbled for the camera and took pictures as I shaded my eyes and watched it soar above us. Native Americans believe the eagle is a divine messenger from God. Its feathers are so sacred a federal law banned ownership to anyone not certified as a Native American.

I tried to think of this bird as a sacred sign, but my heart still raced with fear. It wasn't enough. I planned on backing away at the last moment and waving the three of them onto the plane without me, just like I did with the Ferris wheel. We moved a few more feet forward. There were two families ahead of us now, probably another ten minutes before I could tear the life jacket off me. Suddenly, Zack gasped, and I looked down at him, hoping for a second he was too afraid to board the plane, and I'd have some company.

"Are you okay?"

He nodded and held up his water bottle. "I just forgot to throw this away. Be right back."

He ran toward the restaurants, his fists pumping. He weaved in between the tables and chairs, searching for a garbage can. He passed a few cafés before he stopped in front of a hostess station. He stood in front of the cabinet of drawers. I thought he was waiting for a waitress so he could ask for a garbage can, but he reached out and pulled open the top drawer. He stared down at it for a long moment.

The next family moved ahead and climbed onto their plane. Only one more family left before we boarded.

"Hurry up, Zack," I called and he jerked and slammed the drawer shut. He ran a few feet more to the garbage can at the end of the restaurant. He tossed it in and ran back.

His breath was choppy, his face flushed red, but he was smiling. The last family boarded the plane. We were next. Fear filled me. My heartbeat pounded; I needed a distraction. I turned to Zack and asked him why he'd opened the drawer.

He shrugged. "I don't know. I was looking for a garbage can, but for some reason, I stopped and opened the drawer. And there it was, right on top."

"What?" Lizzie asked.

Zack grinned. "A feather. When I opened the drawer, there was a feather inside. It was huge. It might have even been from an eagle."

Michael closed his eyes and inhaled deeply. "Thank you," he whispered. The three of them nodded, their eyes shining. They believed in this feather. After a moment, I nodded too.

I walked the five or six steps up to the shaky platform. The water lapped over the boards, inching toward my feet. My knees buckled. My hands trembled as I tightened the clasp on my jacket. But I didn't back away. I chose to believe. I boarded the plane with my family as if I carried a fistful of feathers.

I spent the first five minutes staring straight ahead, my fingers clutching my tote bag, listening to the gasps all around me. Finally, I looked out the window at the giant mountains of snow, with deep crevices of sparkling blue. I forgot my fear and leaned forward so I could see more beauty.

Twenty minutes later, we landed in Taku. I walked off the plane, victorious. I pumped my fist into the air. "I did it," I shouted.

Michael grinned. "Was this it? Was this the sign you've been waiting for?"

I shook my head no. I smiled when his shoulders sagged in disappointment. "Don't worry. It's going to be something even bigger than this."

53

We spent the day in Taku, eating salmon and watching a baby bear climb a tree. I had no problems climbing into the seaplane to return to Juneau. We celebrated by walking into town to buy a sweatshirt. We walked several blocks down, trying to get out of the tourist district. I'd told Michael that I was meant to buy something on this trip, something meaningful. I didn't know what at the time, but standing in front of all these stores, I knew.

"We need to buy a totem pole," I said to Michael.

The totem pole is a proud part of Alaskan culture. It takes time and skill to carve one from wood. Each animal is symbolic and stacked together, they work to tell a story. They're meant to reach deep into the roots of the past, and yet standing tall, they stretch into the future.

I've never liked them. Perhaps because totem poles require patience. It takes time to tease out the untold story, to see each animal and understand its symbol.

We walked farther into town, our feet ringing against the wooden sidewalks. The town had a rustic feel to it, with painted signs and saloons with swinging doors. No one sat outside in rocking chairs, and yet, it was easy to picture men rocking back and forth, telling stories they'd never forget while carving those same stories into a piece of wood so others would never forget.

We walked into a souvenir shop, filled with all kinds of wood—rough-hewn wooden shelves, plaques stained to highlight the grain and a row of carved bears and eagles. The man behind the counter flipped his hair out of his eyes, saying hello with a jerk of his chin.

Michael headed toward the eagles while I studied a display of totem poles. Except for music and books, I don't like shopping. Even in high school, when my friends prowled the mall, searching for that perfect jean jacket, I'd be waiting for them at the food court, book in hand.

The selection overwhelmed me, but faint electricity danced across my shoulders, nudging me. *Stay,* it whispered. *Find something.* I was meant to buy one, a symbol of the reasons we were in Alaska. I needed something I could hold and run my fingers over and remember. This is what Brendan wanted.

"Are the totem poles native?" I asked the clerk, trying to narrow down my choices.

"No," he said. He smiled, his eyes crinkling. He wasn't the teen I'd thought, more like in his thirties. "They're from Indonesia." He tilted his head behind him. "I do have some native ones. Those are four to five hundred dollars," he said with a practiced grimace, as if he had no control over the price. He waved toward the cheaper ones, and I nodded. I generally stayed far away from items that were shelved with extra security.

I scanned the Indonesian totems. Each one was about a foot tall, with four or five different figures carved into it, painted with reds, browns and blacks. The animals were mostly birds. Stickers at the bottom of the wood listed the various animals. Michael walked to my side.

"Do you like one?"

I shrugged. His voice held a hopeful question: Is this the magic you're waiting for?

Maybe. But I wasn't sure. I tried to focus, blocking out the noises as Zack and Lizzie pleaded for the most *un*-Alaskan things they could find. They wanted candy or playing cards or lip gloss, nothing that represented Alaska. Maybe they had it right. I was stuck looking at forty totem poles carved with images that meant nothing to me.

Michael picked up one. "How about this one? It has a bear on it. And an eagle."

"I think they all do. Besides, I'm supposed to find one with a story."

"What kind of story?"

I blew out my breath. "I don't know. Just, some kind of story." I wasn't even sure what I meant by *story*, but once I said it, I knew that's what I needed. "I'm looking for one with birds on it. Maybe that's why Zack saw that feather."

I picked up a few more, tracing the details with my finger, but nothing called to me.

"Do you have anything that tells me the story behind the animals?" I asked the clerk. He reached under the counter and handed me a sheet filled with various animals and what their symbols meant. I scanned them quickly; we didn't have much time before our boat left the port. Each animal was associated with a certain quality. *Maybe a pig as a symbol for strength. Or the butterfly for transformation.* But I couldn't buy a butterfly. Halfway down the list, I spotted the raven who's known to be a trickster, the one who likes to play practical jokes and make people laugh with a sly, sarcastic humor.

The clerk had that humor. He reminded me a little of Brendan, with that same mess of hair falling into his eyes and the way he spun lies you didn't mind because you both knew they were lies. He'd been distracting Zack and Lizzie, telling them he played the lead in the latest *Superman* movie. They only half believed him, but they were willing to play along.

Maybe Brendan was the raven. He loved to play tricks and had a devilish laugh that always tempted you to laugh along. Even after he'd died, there were times I could feel him laugh with me. Like the time a few months ago, when Michael and I stood in his room debating whether or not to replace his light. The year before I'd bought a ceiling fan with a light, but Brendan had refused to let me install it. "This light has never failed me," he said. "Why would we replace it?"

But after he died, I'd turned his room into a place where I could write. It was too hot for me. Michael and I stared up at the light Brendan had loved, wondering if we should replace it. And then suddenly, the cover of the light crashed to the floor. We weren't even touching it. The CD player in the hallway started skipping and somehow, the music sounded just like Brendan's laughter. We replaced the light.

Was Brendan laughing at me now, watching me torture myself trying to find the right totem pole? I held one in my hand, touching the eagle and the raven, imagining I could hear his laughter. "This one," I said. If one bird was good, two were even better.

We walked down the street toward our boat. Michael holding my hand, my other hand swinging the bag up and down. Michael kept squeezing my hand, happy, thinking I'd found my sign, but I wasn't so sure. A worm of doubt settled inside me, growing with each step closer to the boat. I didn't say anything.

When we got back to our cabin, the kids spread their souvenirs onto the bed. Michael unwrapped his shirt, holding it up for everyone to admire. It had a bald eagle on it, with just a few feathers sticking to its head. "Bald is beautiful," Michael said, reading the words from his shirt. Zack and Lizzie laughed, not even noticing that I didn't open my bag. I couldn't—it was the wrong totem pole. It hadn't spoken to me like I thought it would. I couldn't even look at it. I shoved it into the suitcase under our bed and tried to forget about it.

54

In Skagway, the four of us slipped on the boots and jackets the tour guides gave us. We heard the whirr of the blades spin before we saw the helicopter fly down from the sky. I stood there, waiting for it to land, my knees shaking, my throat dry. Yesterday's seaplane ride did not lessen my fear, but I was going to board, determined to carry both fear and courage. I was ready to land on a glacier and walk on snow.

The pilot jumped out of the helicopter and pointed to where he wanted us to sit, balancing our weights. He wanted me in the front with him. I pointed to the back, hoping I could sit there and not inches away from the window that made me feel vulnerable. He shook his head.

"Your daughter needs to be there," he said. "She's the smallest."

I climbed into the front, trying not to look at all that glass. Even my feet rested on glass. He gave us headphones, which muffled the roar of the engine. I closed my eyes and hummed along to its pitch, hoping the white noise would cloak my fear.

We moved into the air, a glide more than the jerk I'd expected, and after a few minutes, I felt brave enough to open my eyes. We flew through a canyon of glaciers. Paradise Valley, the guide told us. It was breathtaking. It felt as if we swooped only inches away from the white, jagged peaks, with narrow rivers of blue shining through the layers of ice. The view was worth the fear, and I even looked down at the mountains of ice below my feet. I felt as if I were standing on air.

The ride was short, only fifteen minutes before we floated down onto the glacier. The thick layer of snow muffled the feel and sound of our landing. We climbed out.

Mountains of snow and ice surrounded us.

"It's July, and I'm standing on top of snow," Zack said, laughing as he kicked up a flurry with his boots. Michael reached down and made a snowball. I couldn't seem to move. I tried to catch my breath, but it wasn't fear that made me weak. It was awe.

Lizzie slid her gloved hand into mine. "This feels like heaven," she whispered.

I smiled. She was right. There were no buildings, only white tents scattered in the snow. It was majestic and, for a moment, I had an urge to fall to my knees and offer a prayer of thanks. I was overwhelmed, like the time when I was little and went into New York City and climbed the steps to St. Patrick's Cathedral. I'd knelt in the wooden pew, still feeling the drops of holy water trickling down my neck. I'd looked up, staring in wonder at the carvings in the plaster ceiling.

This glacier was like that cathedral, only with an endless ceiling stretching straight into the sky. This was earth carved into heaven. The Celts called it the thin place, where the two worlds overlapped.

The snow glittered like a stained-glass window. Even the air felt sacred. I let go of Lizzie and turned in a circle, my arms stretched out wide. I moved them up and down, making snow angels in the air. She giggled and copied me.

"Look. There are the dogs." Zack pointed to a pen with puppies crawling over each other. The kids and Michael ran to the dogs, but I stayed in place. I shivered as if I'd dipped my fingers into a font of holy water. I didn't whisper a prayer. I breathed in a silent blessing. I didn't need to pray. The sacred air wrapped itself around me, becoming part of me until my whole body became the prayer.

The glacier was so large that I never saw its edge. It was as if I were standing at the corner of the cliff, ready to dive into the unknown. Each breath filled me with excitement and a certainty that something had shifted inside me. The kids came back with a puppy squirming in Zack's arms.

"His name is Tank," Zack said, kissing the top of his head. "Isn't he the cutest?"

Michael reached over and rubbed his fur. His face was filled with happiness, the kind that was pure, the kind that was a gift from God.

When it was time to again board the helicopter, I bent down and scooped up a handful of snow. I packed it into a ball. I wanted to tuck it inside my pocket, to bring back with me a symbol of everything I'd felt standing on the glacier, even though it would melt before we returned to our cruise ship.

I didn't need it. Standing in the snow, I'd felt a spark of the divine. Since the day my sister had died, I'd denied I was searching for God. I'd watched the priest walk down the street and told myself I couldn't believe in a God that didn't answer my prayers. A God who kept a ledger and added up my entries, trying to decide whether I were worthy or not.

I no longer believed in a God like that, but I didn't know how to let that image go, how to believe in a God that was all around me. It was easier to push Him away, but that day, standing on that glacier, I understood that I'd never stopped searching. Yes, I'd stopped praying, stopped offering words of gratitude, and yet, I searched for the divine everywhere. I hunted for that spark in the songs I sang and each time I ran my fingers over my harp strings. I looked for something more each time I leaned into a tree and listened to the birds sing above me.

Surrounded by mountains of snow, I found this sacred spark that was inside me all along. I was still filled with questions and doubts. Anger still burned inside me, but it was like the grief and joy mixed inside me. I could hold onto both fear and courage at the same time, as well as uncertainty and unwavering belief. And anger and love.

It wasn't that I'd pushed aside one to make room for the other. I didn't banish darkness or doubts. They'd forever be a part of me. But so was the divine. I'd always be filled with yearning, a searching for God.

I knew how to carry it now.

It was rough and dirty, like the banner people once buried at the start of Lent, with the word *Hallelujah* on it. They kept it buried until Easter morning when they dug through the earth and unfolded the banner, brushing off the dirt clinging to the cloth. It was stained and wrinkled, but still they lifted up the Hallelujah and held it to the light.

The glacier had rushed in and carved a holy space, pushing on the edges until I expanded from within and made room for it all. I didn't have the perfect words of a prayer, but it didn't matter because I became the prayer. I felt its Hallelujah inside me. It was a homecoming, and my soul sang the Amen. I believed. I carried it all and held myself up to the light.

55

How do you celebrate the sixteenth birthday of a son who's no longer with you?

I woke up early that morning. The sun was still out; it never seemed to set in Alaska. But the cabin was dark, the kids sleeping in their bunks. Michael was still, his breathing deep and even. I rolled over toward the nightstand. I'd placed my notebook there the night before, making sure my pen was within reach. I'd turned to a fresh page, knowing I'd need to count in the morning, to calculate the number of days without Brendan, the hours, the minutes, maybe even the seconds.

But that morning, I woke up still feeling the peace and happiness from our glacier trip. I stayed in bed for a few minutes, breathing in the quiet. Sixteen years ago, I'd gone into labor in the early morning hours. My contractions had started, my water had broken, and still I'd stayed in bed, watching Michael sleep, filled with anticipation.

I'd held onto that moment, knowing I was going to see my son that day and hold him in my arms. I felt the same way that morning in Alaska, filled with anticipation until the excitement grew and my legs grew restless. I had to get out of bed.

I dressed quickly and grabbed my key to the cabin. I slowly opened the cabin door. Michael stirred. All during the cruise, we'd never adjusted to the time change. We'd wake each morning around four and prowl the ship together, searching for coffee.

I couldn't wait for him this morning. I slipped out the door, knowing he'd follow me. I walked the long hallway, my steps growing faster. I needed to feel the sun against my face. The morning after Brendan died, I'd been so bitter seeing the sun rise, as if nature should have been cloaked in darkness. But now, I needed to see the sun shine. Michael's footsteps sounded behind me, but I didn't slow down. I moved faster.

"Linda, wait," Michael called behind me. His voice was raw. Broken. But I couldn't stop I didn't even turn around. I moved into a half jog until the hallway ended and I pushed through the doors, stopping only when I felt the wind stir against me. I closed my eyes and lifted my face to the sun, feeling the heat spread against my cheeks. I smiled.

Michael opened the door, jerking to a stop when he saw my smile. "Why didn't you wait for me?" And then, "Don't you know what today is?"

Of course I did. But I wasn't filled with the sadness I'd expected. I had a sense of purpose, a mission I couldn't ignore. I grabbed his hands.

"Today is going to be a good day."

He shrugged a little and blew out his breath. "Really?"

"Really."

The ship had slowed down and was floating toward the dock of Ketchikan. I pointed to the town, to the rows of colorful buildings built into the mountain. I'd read in the brochure that the town name meant Eagle Spreads Its Wings. That's how I felt, as if I were ready to take flight and soar high into the sky.

"There," I said, pointing to Ketchikan. "We need to go into town."

Shivers of excitement ran through my body. "It's going to be okay. I know it." I reached out and wiped away the tears trailing down his cheek. "We're going to find magic today. You'll see." I felt it with every cell inside my body.

He leaned into the palm of my hand, resting his cheek there for a few minutes while the boat eased its way into the dock.

"Is it a feeling?" he asked softly.

I smiled. "More than a feeling."

He nodded. The ship blared a long, low horn that sounded like laughter. I grabbed his hand. "C'mon," I said, pulling him with me. "We have to wake the kids and get off this boat."

For a second, I looked back at the town of Ketchikan. We'd already booked a tour for the day, a boat ride through the Mystic Fjords. It had seemed like the perfect trip for Brendan's birthday. Standing in the mist gave me a sense of wonders unseen, like staring at the day-time sky knowing the hidden stars were still out there. But the day before, I'd made Michael cancel the trip, feeling that we were meant to do something different. I didn't know what, though, not until I stood there on deck and felt the sun and wind on me. I knew exactly what we were going to do that day. I wasn't sure what I'd find, but it would be something I could hold in my hand, something that would tell my story.

I smiled. "We're going shopping."

I was patient for the first hour in Ketchikan. We walked past the giant souvenir shop and explored the town. We shook our heads no at trying reindeer hot dogs. Zack continued his quest to find the perfect fish and chips and we wandered around the streets, watching salmon jump out of the water, until I finally nodded at Michael and we turned around and walked back to the store.

It was huge, jammed with all things Alaskan. We'd seen them all before; the sweatshirts, wooden bears and packets of sourdough bread mix. And, of course, the glass shelves of totem poles. I ignored it at first, skirting the store, trying to see if jewelry sparked anything within me. *Nothing.* I walked back to the front of the store and stared at the display, shaking my head. I didn't want to buy another totem pole. I'd already shoved one under my bed. But I was pushed toward the display by something I couldn't resist. I crouched over the shelves, my muscles tight. There were so many of them. None of them looked right.

I blew out my breath and backed up. I walked to the opposite end of the store, where Zack and Lizzie flipped through stacks of sweatshirts and pajamas. Zack held up a onesie. "Let's get this for Sean." I nodded yes.

I'd picked out a pair of socks when Michael came up to me, his arms filled with T-shirts.

He smiled. "They have totem poles. I think I'm feeling Brendan by them."

I sighed. "Yeah, I know. He's there. I just can't figure out which one I'm supposed to buy. It's kinda pissing me off." I had to go back. I had only a few more minutes before Zack and Lizzie would ask to leave. I shoved the socks into Michael's hands and stomped back to the display. I took a deep breath, my eyes narrowing until all the totem poles blended together. I reached out blindly and picked one up. *Nothing.* I reached for another. *Nope.* I closed my eyes and counted to three. *Please, Brendan. Help me find the right one. Or, at least tell me I'm supposed to buy a sweatshirt.*

I reached out, my eyes closed, my fingers fumbling. I touched one. Still nothing. But then, my hand brushed against the wood of another totem pole. I froze, feeling that sacred wind whisper to me. *This is it.*

I picked it up, drawing it to me slowly. I didn't even look at it. I cupped it with both hands against my heart, smiling at Michael when he walked up to me. "This is it," I said. "I finally found it."

I held it against me for a long time. The electric shivers of joy from this morning returned, but also a deep river of peace flowing inside me. *This is what I was meant to find.*

"It feels like magic," I whispered.

"Can I see?" Michael asked.

I opened my hands and held out the totem pole. It was a little taller than my hand, carved in brown wood and painted in red and black. Michael touched one of the wings.

"It's an eagle," I said.

"It's beautiful. I know you wanted one with a bird. What else is carved into it?"

I squinted at it. I'd chosen this one from a feeling, not from its carvings. "I'm not really sure." I pointed to the figure under the eagle. "I think this is a person. I have no clue what's under him." I flipped it over, looking for the sticker identifying the figures. There wasn't one, only a *Made in Alaska* sticker and an artist's signature. A card was tied with a gold string around the eagle's neck. I opened it, expecting to see the author's bio. I gasped.

"It's a story," I said, tears blurring my eyes. "A story about a mother bear who's lost her son." I shifted so Michael could read the card with me.

The Legend of Bear Mother tells a story about a mother bear who lost her son. For days the crashing of the brush could be heard as Bear Mother searched for her lost cub. Knowing he had the ability to transform, she was afraid she might not recognize him. Eagle came to her and told her of a brave new man who was to be trained to lead the neighboring village. He beckoned her to come at once to view the ongoing ceremonies.

She follows Eagle to the village in hopes that this new brave man could help her find her son. As they approach, Bear Mother is alerted to a familiar sound. They quicken their pace until before them stands the chief to be, who Bear Mother recognizes at once to be her son."

"It's me," I whispered. "I'm the mother bear. This is my story." The story of a mother who knew that her son could transform into something else, only she was afraid she wouldn't recognize his spirit. But the eagle showed her the way.

"That's what the bird meant the day it walked into our house," I said. "You were right. It was carrying a message."

I traced the curve of its wings. *This is my story.* I was finally ready to listen to the whispers within and all around me, knowing that I'd find my son, whether he transformed into a sparrow or song. This was a story that would stay with me forever, just like my son.

Michael wrapped his arms around me and rested his head against my shoulder, and together we read the story again.

Grace Note

A note that comes before the melody note. It's a quick note, not meant to change the tempo or alter the rhythm of the melody. It can clash with the melody note, just a bit, like a speck of dust. But the dissonance adds color, like a sprinkling of fairy dust that makes the melody shine.

It's a little spark that says: *Listen. This is beauty. This is light.*

This is grace.

Postlude

It's a few months after our trip to Alaska, and I'm at our church, standing on the chancel with my harp, looking out at the congregation. Rev. Rick is at the back of the sanctuary, excited that I finally brought my harp to church. "I'm going to try," I said to Argaille before the service started. She held up her finger, shaking it. "Don't try. Just do."

Michael and the kids are at a football game scheduled months ago. I told them it was okay to go, that it would make me less nervous. "Besides," Zack said. "We've heard you play the song dozens of times now."

I've only played for them. And the choir. I played and sang for them a few days ago. But this was harder. I'm not sure I can play, much less sing, even though I was the one who asked to do this.

My parents are in the pew. It's been a little over a year since they were in this church for Brendan's funeral. They came today to hear me sing with the choir. Of course, they came early.

"I didn't realize you're singing a solo. We'll leave," my mother said when she saw the tears in my eyes. "If it's too hard for you to have us here, we'll leave."

But I shook my head. I wasn't afraid of my tears anymore. I smile at them now, even though my legs shake, and my mouth is dry. I thought I was ready, but now I'm not so sure. I search for Dina sitting with the congregation. I need her nod. Our eyes meet. She nods back at me. My palm brushes over the wood as I reach for my harp. My fingers tremble. I touch my necklace, feeling for the bear carved in onyx. I bought it after I found the totem pole. I wanted something I could wear around my neck, something that made me remember the totem pole that sits on my desk at home.

My right hand rests on the curve of my harp, my left brushes down the soundboard. I can't push away my fear; I need to just keep on going.

"Today, I want to sing *Amazing Grace,*" I say. My throat is tight, my words broken. My mother smiles, and I give a small one back. My father sits up straight, his shoulders back, as if he's willing his strength into me, the same way he did when we sang the hymns at Brendan's funeral. *Daddy fix.* I take a deep breath.

"Most of you know I've struggled with playing in front of anyone this past year. But today . . . well today, I'm going to try." I stop for a moment and turn to Argaille who sat only a few feet away from me. *Don't try. Just do.*

"It's not going to be perfect," I warn. "But then, that's the definition of grace. This song is about God's love." I thought of the day when the church gathered around us, their hands linked together as they held onto our faith. "God loves us. Even when we don't believe. Even when we fall down and make mistakes. God's love . . . well, it's always there, no matter what we believe, no matter what we do. It's there. That is grace."

I sit down and reach for my harp. I pull it back, hugging it to me. Its gentle weight rests against my shoulder. I take a deep breath, listening in the silence. I pluck a D and then another, hoping to ground myself. The sound waves wrap around the strings until they vibrate and sing their own melody that floats upward. Even in my fear, I smile, listening to the notes climb up a ladder, reaching for the heavens. I feel a whisper move across me.

He's here.

Brendan is behind me, reaching for my strings, cradling himself around me, my reminder that a ladder moves in both directions. Heaven and earth.

You got this, he seems to whisper. *You got this.*

I take a deep breath, my arms weightless as they float to the strings. My fingers fumble. I play the introduction but I'm not ready when it's time to sing. The lump lodged in my throat is too great. I don't give up. I slow down and start over. I start to sing. I cringe at the sound of my voice. It's weak. Breathless. I don't stop.

I once was lost, but now I am found.

My voice cracks on the word found, but I don't stop playing, I don't stop singing. This is my broken Hallelujah. I rock on the bench, reaching for the bass notes and start the second verse. I keep my eyes on the strings. The carpet beneath me is red and blurs out all my red strings. It doesn't matter; I don't need to see. I know how to reach for invisible strings now.

That grace appeared the hour I first believed.

My voice is still thin, but I don't stop. I believe in the light now. I no longer hide behind the glass, too afraid to open my heart. I believe in birds and the feathers they leave behind. I believe in Brendan and the music we make in my harp. I believe in a God that walks with me in sadness and joy, anger and love.

On the third verse, I start to sway even more, lost in the flow of the song. There's tears and laughter in my song, two of the three things kings required from their harpists. The third—dreams—were what had always escaped me.

I fall asleep each night begging for them. I want to hear just a tiny scrap of Brendan's laughter or that giggle he made when I squeezed his knee. I want to watch him tilt his head or stare out the window, lost in his own world. I wake each morning, disappointed.

But now I know I was looking in the wrong place.

My dreams come to me during the day, when I sit behind my harp. Something more than melody, harmony, and rhythm is in its sound. There's magic. I wrap my arms around strings and wood pulsing with power and press it against my heart. I don't just hear each note, but feel them flow through me. They feel like Brendan and, yes, a God that never left me, a God that walks with me even in my anger, even in my doubts. They're wrapped up together in the music, a divine mystery that defies logic.

I don't need words to explain it. My son is in my harp. He's everywhere. He's been with me since the day that bird hopped into our house and waited for me to believe. He's in the songs Michael brings home. He's with me as I sing my final words in front of the congregation. My voice is only a whisper now. Broken. Still, I sing.

And grace will lead me home.

This is my dream.

Acknowledgments

*A*nd Still the Bird Sings transformed from a pile of notebooks and scribbled memories into a book. There are so many people who helped me along the way.

I started my writing journey at The Writers Circle. Their classes and feedback helped shape this book. Special thanks to Vinessa DiSousa, whose guidance and editing helped make this a much better book. And to *Hippocampus Magazine* and editor Donna Talarico who published my harp essay, "Strings." A version of it appears in this book. It was my first publication and sparked the beginnings of this book.

I'm so grateful to Windy Lynn Harris whose class made me feel like a real writer. She gave me the courage and confidence to finally submit my work. And to Brooke Warner and Lauren Wise at She Writes Press for guiding me in this process and for creating a platform where our stories could be told.

Thank you to all my friends and neighbors, who brought me casseroles and hope and listened to all my stories (more than once!) Special thanks to Christine Meissner who read this book in its early form.

Thank you to Rev. Rick and my UPC family. You showed me what faith could look like. And to Argaille and the choir, who welcomed me when I could barely sing a note. I don't think I could have found my voice without you.

My love and gratitude to my parents who knew firsthand our pain and walked with us every step of the way. And to my mother-in-law, Fran, who tried desperately to ease our sorrow in any way she could.

I'm grateful for my brothers and sisters on both sides. Your help was invaluable. How lucky Michael and I are to be surrounded by such a loving family. They gave us love and strength and supported us all.

Brendan adored his cousins—Kaitlyn, Jimmy, Sean, Deanna, AJ, Sami, Jake, Ally, David, Erica, Barrie, Jaime, George, Ruth, Allison, and Jonathan. He loved spending time with you all—sharing meals, playing marathon Monopoly games, playing pranks, making silly videos, and hanging out on the couch watching movies.

And always to Michael, Brendan, Zack, and Lizzie who inspired me to write this book. Your stories fill my heart forever.

About the Author

Linda Broder is a writer and meditative musician living in New Jersey. She finds stories everywhere—from the songs of birds to the whispers of trees to the music in her harp and piano. She believes everyone has a story to tell and teaches creative classes that are a soulful blend of music, meditation, poetry, and prompts.

She's obsessed with crystals and singing bowls and reading while taking four-hour baths. She believes a home should always be filled with music, books, and laughter.

SELECTED TITLES FROM SHE WRITES PRESS

She Writes Press is an independent publishing company founded to serve women writers everywhere. Visit us at www.shewritespress.com.

Blinded by Hope: One Mother's Journey Through Her Son's Bipolar Illness and Addiction by Meg McGuire. $16.95, 978-1-63152-125-6
A fiercely candid memoir about one mother's roller coaster ride through doubt and denial as she attempts to save her son from substance abuse and bipolar illness.

Breathe: A Memoir of Motherhood, Grief, and Family Conflict by Kelly Kittel. $16.95, 978-1-93831-478-0
A mother's heartbreaking account of losing two sons in the span of nine months—and learning, despite all the obstacles in her way, to find joy in life again.

Notes After Midnight: How I Outlasted My Teenagers, One Mistake at a Time by Carol Richmond. $16.95, 978-1-63152-633-6
In this haunting memoir, Carol Richmond relives the ten-year experience of raising three children on her own after her ex-husband abandons his paternal responsibilities. One of her sons attempts suicide, the other fails academically, and her daughter is sexually abused by a trusted acquaintance—yet the family endures, because they must.

Suspended Sentence: A Memoir by Janice Morgan
$16.95, 978-1-63152-644-2
Janice Morgan faces her worst nightmare when her son is arrested for drug charges and wanton endangerment with a handgun. When she learns that he can have his sentence diverted if he completes the drug court program, she reflects on what it will take to avoid falling back into codependent patterns—and truly help her son.

The Red Ribbon: A Memoir of Lightning and Rebuilding After Loss by Nancy Freund Bills. $16.95, 978-1-63152-573-5
In the summer of 1994, a lightning accident on the coast of Maine leaves Nancy Bills's son critically hurt and her husband dead. In this inspiring memoir, Bills captures the shock and grief that follow this unusual and devastating loss, and shares how she and her sons find the strength to recover from it.